Praise
Let's Save

Let's Save America is both passionate and inspiring, two adjectives seldom associated with finance-oriented writings.

In addition to making me wish I were 20 years younger so I could apply what I learned from the book and retire while I'm still young, the authors manage to make me believe - truly believe - I can still make a significant improvement in the financial outlook of my fast-approaching "golden years."

Perhaps more importantly, reading this book made me want to buy a copy for each of the children in my family, and pay them a dollar a year for every page they read - if they agree to put it where it'll earn compound interest. This kind of start could give them some wonderful economic choices in adulthood, and set them free to focus their creative energies on causes that all too often fall by the wayside because we're all too busy trying to make ends meet and build our nest eggs.

If we were given two options: a thousand bucks to give each young person in this great country of ours, or one copy each of *Let's Save America*, I think the book would do more good. This isn't just one investment broker's ideas committed to paper; this is potentially the start of a long overdue economic revolution.

Dr. Karen E. N. Hayes

It's hard to imagine a self-improvement book with a broader appeal or a more compelling message than *Let's Save America*.

Authors Bradley Dugdale, Jr., and Donald Ferrell have pooled their talents to produce an easy-to-follow blueprint for personal financial success. Sure, there are other books that offer hints on how to manage money, but this one should be required reading for every high school senior, and yet also has value for the wealthy and worldly-wise.

Let's Save America borrows from no less a sage than Benjamin Franklin. It is a fresh retelling of Franklin's simple but incredibly powerful message about the time-value of money. Franklin knew that money invested wisely over time produces almost magical results. Dugdale and Ferrell know the value of compound interest, too. Unlike Franklin, they also know that today, most of America has forgotten this fact. Indeed, Americans today are spenders rather that savers. Wooed by relentless assaults from advertisers, and unaware that easy credit is the "dark side" of the compound interest formula, Americans are declaring bankruptcy in record numbers.

Let's Save America is a sobering look at the social consequences of our love affair with conspicuous consumption and our aversion for a sensible program of saving and investing. The book reveals both common financial pitfalls and common sense ways to avoid them. Whether you're well on your way to financial independence or can't balance your checkbook, you'll find *Let's Save America* both interesting and rewarding.

Ben Franklin also said, "Remember that time is money." The time I spent reading *Let's Save America* couldn't have been better invested; what I already knew was well worth reading again, and the new information I gained from the book is priceless. If you've ever worried about your financial future, and who hasn't, you'll find peace of mind in the pages of *Let's Save America*. Take this book home with you and read it from cover to cover before you open another credit card solicitation!

Steve Schenk

LET'S SAVE AMERICA

Nine Lessons To Financial Success

*How to use the power of compound interest
to accumulate your retirement fortune
in nine simple, understandable lessons.*

Bradley Dugdale, Jr.

Donald M. Ferrell

Printed and bound in the United States of America. No part of this book may be reproduced in any form or by any electronic or mechanical means including information storage and retrieval systems without permission in writing from the publisher and authors, except by a reviewer, who may quote brief passages in a review. Printed by Unique Printing Services, Inc., 7600 Mineral Dr., Suite 600, P.O. Box 2027, Coeur d'Alene, ID. 83816-2027.

Library of Congress Control Number: 00-090496

ISBN: 0-9700067-0-5

This book is printed on acid-free paper.

Books are available at special quantity discounts to use as premiums and sales promotions, or for use in training programs. For more imformation, please write to Denali Publishing Co., 9493 N. Govrnment Way, Hayden, ID 83835,

(208) 762-7602.

ABOUT THE AUTHORS

Bradley Dugdale, Jr., a University of Montana graduate, has been employed as a financial consultant at a large regional investment firm for 18 years. In 1990, he was named Vice President/Branch Manager. He was promoted to Senior Vice President/Branch Manager of the office in 1996. For eight consecutive years he has served as a member of the firms' Chairman's Advisory Council. His community service includes serving as president of the North Idaho College Foundation, a position he continues to hold, and as a member of the foundation's finance committee. He successfully chaired the Coeur d'Alene All-America City Committee in 1990. He presently is serving, or has served, on numerous community committees and functions.

Donald M. Ferrell worked as a journalist in the newspaper industry and as a partner-owner of a national magazine. He also taught newspaper and magazine reporting and writing classes at two major universities, and served as director of student publications at Washington State University. He now lives in Idaho and writes non-fiction, fiction and poetry. He earned a Bachelor of Arts in journalism at San Diego State University, and a Master of Arts in journalism at the University of Missouri.

The investment principles, strategies and concepts presented in this book do not reflect the policies, or express the opinion, of any securities firm. Neither this book, nor any opinion expressed herein, should be construed as an offer to buy or sell any securities. Any strategies presented should not be implemented without first consulting a trusted investment advisor, certified public accountant or attorney.

Authors' Notes

Let's Save America has seen a long developmental process, and we wish to thank contributors for their ongoing support of the project. We are most grateful, of course, for their expert contributions, which are the essence of the work. Their names are listed after this brief introduction.

I would like to thank my wife, Shariae Dugdale, for being my patient companion, and my sons, Bradley and Chase, for becoming my inspiration. My deep appreciation also goes to my father, Bradley Dugdale, for passing to me his work ethic and integrity.

Don and I are grateful for the sharp eyes and careful copyediting the book received from our mutual friends, Steve Schenk, and his wife, Gretchen Berning. Thanks also to Karen Hayes and Tom Brooke. We deeply appreciate their faith in our work and their helpful guidance.

Thanks are due to my friend, Doug Ratelle, for helping me embrace the truth.

Our gratitude goes to those who offered help and guidance, such as Dennis Osterdock and Gary Waters, who helped mold this project, and Rick McGee, for helping us reach a technological edge. Others are Kate Absec, a trusted pal and my Rock of Gibraltar. I also want to recognize Ali Shute for her creativity, and Alan and Judy Brown for their encouragement.

Finally, my thanks to Don Ferrell and his wife, Joyce, for without their help this would never have happened.

Bradley Dugdale, Jr.

First and foremost, I want to thank Bradley for the opportunity to participate in the project. His enthusiasm and heartfelt faith are uplifting and appreciated.

Along with those named by Bradley, I want to thank my talented wife, Joyce Kay Ferrell, who read and copyedited the manuscript in each full draft. She made helpful and perceptive editorial comments throughout the project, and passed to me her limitless moral support.

Joan Brogan deserves a special word of appreciation for her strong backing and encouragement. She has, without hesitation, given me guidance in other writing endeavors.

Special thanks go the the distant but consistent support I receive from my two children, Donald M. Ferrell II, in Columbia, Missouri, and Sharon Lee Harris, in Hattiesburg, Mississippi.

Donald M. Ferrell

Contents

Preface

Directly or indirectly, every theme in this book connects to the phenomenon of compound interest, the most dynamic, safe and soundest way for many of us to become financially independent. Compound interest can work for you, too, if you follow the formula and let the element of time stockpile earned interest on top of earned interest.

My goal in writing this book is to objectively expose and educate as many people as possible to the power of compound interest.

I first heard of compound interest while enrolled in a University of Montana

finance class in 1978. Back then, I had a hot, new calculator called an HP12C that could calculate future values, and I'd use it to tally compound interest rates. While attending college, I had a dream to become a millionaire—an amount which, in 1978, was considered a lot of money.

I plugged in $85 a month and then, using a 12 percent interest rate compounded monthly for forty years. It amazed me that the total amounted to a million dollars.

This calculation was astounding. Here I was, twenty years of age, saying, "wait a second." I rechecked my figures three or four times and it always came out the same. I used someone else's calculator to make sure mine wasn't broken, and it confirmed my figures. I just couldn't believe it was possible to produce a million dollars on $85 dollars a month. If it's that simple, why wasn't everybody a millionaire?

The new knowledge of compound interest made me an aggressive saver. The formula is a simple, easy to understand mathematical calculation that gets rave reviews from financial advisors and intelligent investors everywhere.

Simply put, the rule is a sum of money (principal) wisely invested at a good, steady (rate) return, left untouched over a long period (time)—years and years of time. That's all there is to it. As the yearly returns take advantage of compound interest, your account becomes more and more valuable.

In 1982, I went to work for an investment firm and the formula of compound interest came back in my life in a different manner. Instead of just using the formula, I would teach the practice of compound interest to others so they could experience financial growth.

I was excited when I could use the miracle of compounding to help other people. The first thing I did was run out to recruit all my friends. I explained the concept and encouraged them to save. After all, if I intended to become wealthy, I wanted all my friends to have the same opportunity.

I felt very successful; I had enrolled about twenty-five people, each saving $85 a month from their checkbooks through automatic deductions. Even though I had done a lot of work and opened twenty-five new accounts, the volume wasn't adequate and gross commissions were next to nothing.

Before long my boss told me that I should look for clients who had attained more substantial wealth if I wanted to stay in the investment business. I still felt very passionate about the process, but if I wanted to continue as a financial advisor, I knew I'd have to find people who had already accumulated wealth, not those in the process of collecting it.

Too few Americans comprehend that only a small percentage of our citizens achieve financial independence. Therefore, when you see the financial service industry's advertisements, they're directed toward that very small segment of society—the people who have already gained wealth.

Unfortunately, the very fact that the industry reaches out to the people with money makes it difficult to help those without it, and they are the ones who really need to learn the principles that lead to independence.

What's really bothersome is that not enough Americans have knowledge of the formula and no one is educating this country about the miracle of compound interest.

Why is this happening? Why are only a small percentage of Americans retiring financially independent?

There aren't any simple answers to that question, but I'll offer some suggestions that might explain why more Americans should embrace compound interest as a sure-fire way to financial success.

The Hundredth Monkey

After almost two decades in the financial service industry, during America's most prosperous times, I have experienced and executed the compound interest formula. My wife and I started using the formula 18 years ago, and after fifteen years began to benefit from some of the financial freedom it afforded us. Now we want others to experience this same financial freedom, too.

Through this book and the Let's Save America (LSA) Foundation, we will use the hundredth monkey principle (critical mass) to spread the word about compound interest. Over time, I want each reader, as you realize the prosperity of compound interest, to become a teacher. The teacher will share the benefit of the formula with others.

The hundredth monkey is a great example of critical mass. In the early 1950s, some scientists were observing a group of monkeys on a distant island.

> Two men working as a team will produce more than three men working as individuals.
> President William McKinley

As part of their research, scientists fed the monkeys a diet of sweet potatoes by dropping them on the sandy ground. The monkeys liked the sweet potatoes but found the sand displeasing.

A young monkey soon came along and found a solution: She washed her sweet potatoes in a nearby stream. The monkey soon passed her discovery on to her mother, and a lot of her monkey friends caught on, and passed it to others in the tribe.

This cultural innovation spread, and by the late 1950s, all the young monkeys had learned to wash the sand off their sweet potatoes.

Over time, some of the adult monkeys caught on by imitating their children. Others kept eating sweet potatoes flavored with sand, despite what the gritty stuff was doing to their teeth.

In late 1959, something startling happened at a time when an unknown number of monkeys were regularly visiting the stream to wash their sweet potatoes before eating them.

We don't know the precise number of monkeys who had adopted this process, but let's deduce that the total added up to ninety-nine.

Let's further conclude that a little later that day the hundredth monkey took its sweet potato down to the stream and swirled it around in the water before eating it. By late afternoon most of the tribal monkeys had started to wash their sweet potatoes. The next day all the monkeys washed their sweet potatoes before eating.

The added energy of the hundredth monkey somehow created a visual picture and thought pattern that convinced those coming later to wash the sand off their sweet potatoes, too.

I believe the hundredth monkey principle (critical mass) will work for the compound interest formula. After a while, when a certain number achieves an awareness of the rule, this new perception will be communicated from mind to mind, and people will look at its benefits. It will then be accepted as a method of moving all Americans to a higher financial level.

Although the exact numbers may differ, when only a limited amount of people know of a new way, it will remain the conscious property of these people for a period of time. Eventually LSA will grow to a critical mass, when enough of us will hear, adopt and use the new way as our own. The knowledge will grow to where a lone person tips the scale, and, like a seesaw, that person's single weight joins the critical mass of LSA and moves the heavier mass to the ground while sending the lighter mass into the air.

In a sense, that's what this book is about—a campaign to educate the young and old to the power of compound interest. We want to impact a million people. Our aim is to reach enough readers who in turn will spread the shrouded word of compound interest to their family, friends and neighbors.

When people discipline themselves and follow the formula, they will become wealthy. Many will become millionaires.

As a group of people gain the knowledge and feel the benefit of compound interest, the formula will create a positive and substantial impact on society.

The Maslow Hierarchy of Needs

The noted behavioral scientist Abraham H. Maslow wrote that people conduct themselves depending on their real or perceived needs. He said human beings order their lives to meet a hierarchy of needs.

Five basic needs are described in Maslow's hierarchy of needs. He placed them in order of their strength—physiological needs, safety needs, belonging and love needs, self-esteem needs, and self-actualization needs. An individual must satisfy each lower need before he or she can become aware of or develop the capacity to fulfill the needs above it.

Presented in more detail, Maslow's need hierarchy is as follows:

Physiological needs, such as hunger and sleep, are dominant and are the basis of motivation. These needs must be satisfied in order to move upward in the hierarchy. For example, people who suffer from poor nutrition generally become lethargic and withdrawn, thus lowering their learning potential.

Safety needs represent the importance of security, protection, stability, freedom from fear and anxiety, and the need for structure and limits. For example, those who fear school, or peers, or the reactions of others have their well being and safety needs threatened.

Love and belongingness needs refers to the need for family and friends. Healthy, motivated people wish to avoid feelings of loneliness and isolation. People who feel alone, not part of the group, or who lack any sense of belongingness usually have poor relationships with others, which can affect their achievement in life.

Esteem needs, or a feeling of self-worth. Humans want to feel valuable not only to themselves, but to others. Esteem needs refer to the reaction of others to us as individuals and also to our opinion of ourselves.

Self-actualization needs. By self-actualization needs, Maslow referred to the human tendency that in spite of the lower needs being satisfied, we feel restless unless we are doing what we think we are capable of doing. For instance, singers must sing, writers must write, artists must draw or paint.

Listed in that order, Maslow claimed that depending on where we are positioned on the five-step hierarchy often determines how we react to a particular situation.

Maslow claimed that because of their circumstances, some individuals find it hard to satisfy lower order needs, yet fulfilling lower order needs help them realize greater psychological health and self-actualization.

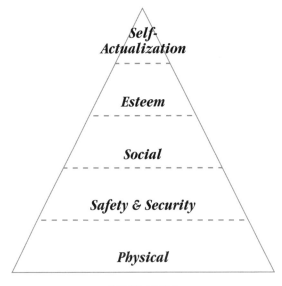

MASLOW'S
HIERARCHY OF NEEDS

Maslow's hierarchy makes sense; it's definitely hard to think of others if you're hungry. If your basic needs aren't taken care of, your primary thoughts and actions will focus on survival.

Once your survival needs are met, you can think about your role in society. As you integrate through society you have the opportunity to develop your own self-worth. Self-worth moves to self-actualization, which is maximizing one's talents and pursuing one's life passions.

The Bell curve is a popular measuring device often used by statisticians. The Bell curve illustrates the frequency of the item that is measured. The curve resembles the outline of a Bell—thus the name, Bell curve.

Let's measure the U.S. population using a "financial Bell curve." When we analyze the financial Bell curve, let's ask a few questions using Maslow's hierarchy of needs as a backdrop.

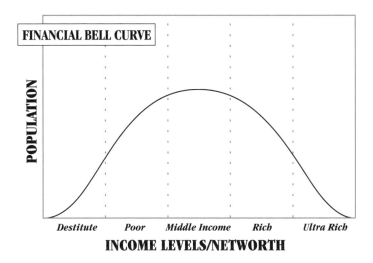

Which side of the curve has higher divorce rates?

Which side of the curve engages in more criminal activity?

Which side has more stress and health related issues?

Which side of the curve would engage in get rich quick schemes or scams?

Since this book is about the power of compound interest, let's place the compound interest chart over the financial Bell curve.

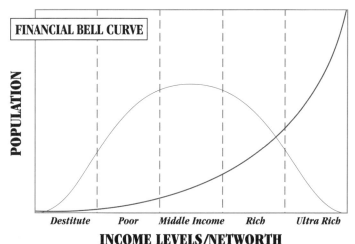

INCOME LEVELS/NETWORTH

The graph of compound interest illustrates the magic of **P x R x T**. The line representing principal starts low, but as interest and time are added, the line moves up to the right. The longer the principal stays in the formula, the higher the ascent.

To make this more interesting, let's add Maslow's hierarchy to the financial Bell curve. In essence, let's tip over the triangle and add Maslow's hierarchy to the financial Bell curve.

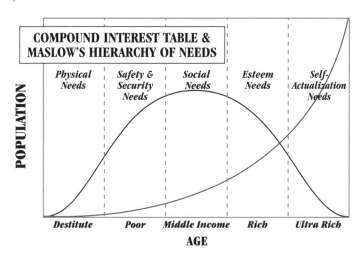

My personal experience is that the longer I used the formula of compound interest, the further I progressed through Maslow's hierarchy of needs. Over the past twenty years I observed others that had accumulated assets and noticed the same tendencies that I had experienced.

There is a strong correlation between net-worth and self-worth. The longer investors use compound interest, the higher they move through Maslow's hierarchy and the more they think of others rather than themselves. The personal gratification of helping others is hard to describe.

But what's going on in today's society? In some states and communities, crime rates are on the rise and so are the divorce rates. Get rich quick schemes are a dime a dozen. People are lining up to get rich through lotteries and lawsuits.

Our country is experiencing a financial shift in the Bell curve.

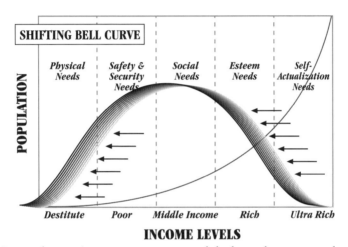

More and more Americans continue to slide down the compound interest charts and as a result, experience more physical, safety and security needs. The trend of descent seems to be accelerating at an alarming rate.

What Causes the Shift?

Over the past two years the financial press has noticed the decline in America's savings rate. Although the index needs to be recalculated for retirement plans, the savings rate drop is still a perilous trend.

There appears to be a strong correlation between advertising through the medium of television and the change in attitudes toward consumer credit over the past thirty years.

If you look at a graph of the distribution of television from 1959 to present, and impose it on top of the U.S. savings rate, it depicts an interesting trend between advertising and saving.

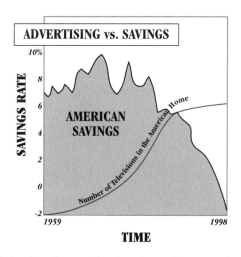

ADVERTISING vs. SAVINGS

AMERICAN SAVINGS

SAVINGS RATE

Number of Televisions in the American Home

1959 — 1998

TIME

Number of Commercials Watched by the Average Child

3-4,000	per month
36-48,000	per year
720,000	By Age 18
1,440,000	By Age 36
2,880,000	By Age 54

It's hard to dispute the fact that television advertising works. The advertising industry spends $186 billion dollars a year to convince us to purchase things. Each day, Americans are exposed to 12 billion display ads, 2.7 million radio commercials and more than 305,000 television commercials. On the average, American households watch seven hours of television a day.

Advertisers pride themselves on knowing ahead of time what their customers want. With televisions in 98 percent of American households—many with two or more—it's an advertiser's wildest dream.

The American public willingly buys electronic billboards (television sets), and places them in their homes. Networks provide free entertainment, in exchange for viewing advertisements. What started in America quickly spread worldwide.

It's estimated that the average American child watches 3,000 to 4,000 television commercials a month. That's 36,000 to 48,000 commercials a year!

By the time a child reaches 18 years of age, he or she watched 720,000 television commercials. The figure balloons to 1.44 million by age 36. And 2.88 million television commercials by age 54.

Does advertising work? Yes, no question about it—from expensive sunglasses to designer blue jeans, to luxury cars. Try driving past McDonald's at lunch or dinner with young children in the car.

Do you think there's a link between advertising and the savings rate?

Consumer Credit

Benjamin Franklin spoke these words on July 7, 1757:

But poverty often deprives a man of all spirit and virtue; 'tis hard for an empty bag to stand upright, and…then (the) borrower is a slave to the lender.

Thirty years ago attitudes on borrowing money were completely different. After the depression, debt was despised. People paid cash for everything. Apparently, we have short memories.

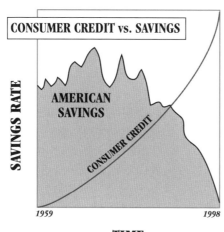

CONSUMER CREDIT vs. SAVINGS

SAVINGS RATE

AMERICAN SAVINGS

CONSUMER CREDIT

1959   1998

TIME

Credit Cards:

- The average American has 8 - 10 credit cards.
- Card issuers send out 3.5 billion solicitations per year.
- Americans currently hold 455 billion dollars in credit card debt.
- In 1998, 1.4 million people declared bankruptcy.

The American economy is based on consumer debt. We're constantly urged to buy, buy, and buy. Buy big and buy often.

The 1980s were a decade of readily available credit and seductive pressures exhorting us to buy goods and services at an unparalleled rate. As a result, many Americans were led into an almost bottomless pit of insurmountable debt overload. The same trend of the '80s continued through the 1990s.

It is not unusual for a debtor's home to have a first mortgage and a home equity loan. Some home equity loans allow people to borrow more than the value of the property. Is this good planning?

Because cars depreciate at a rate faster than their payoff, the loan balance on an automobile is often as much or more than the vehicle is worth in the market place.

It is not surprising that many debtors find themselves in a position of "…being relegated to a lifetime of destitution or the functional equivalent of financial indentured servitude from which they can never hope to recover." (House Report No. 103-835)

It's little wonder that when burdened with insurmountable debt, many borrowers often feel angry with themselves, their spouses, and even their

21

creditors. Many are embarrassed and feel like failures, damaging their feelings of self-worth.

The average American has eight to ten credit cards. Credit card issuers send out 3.5 billion solicitations a year. Ever count how many solicitations you receive? It seems like I get half of them.

In 1998, consumer debt reached an all time high, totaling into the trillions of dollars. Credit card debt went through the roof to a tune of $455 billion. Many consumers suffer from minimum payment syndrome (MPS). Minimum payment syndrome pyramids consumer debt until any short term financial hardship produces disastrous results. The final repercussion is an increase in the number of families filing bankruptcy.

Bankruptcies in America in 1998 reached 1,398,182, setting a record for the third straight year. Credit and bankruptcy are closely related. Many American families are so deeply in debt that they are within two paychecks of financial ruin. In other words, if they miss receiving two paychecks in a row, they would be staring into the eyes of bankruptcy.

Total bankruptcies are up 84.2 percent since 1990, when they totaled 782,960. Since 1980, more than 12.8 million households have declared bankruptcy.

Personal bankruptcy filings drove the increase, representing 96.9 percent of all filings in 1998. In all, personal bankruptcies are up 94.7 percent since 1990.

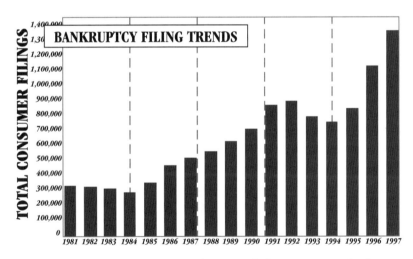

Samuel J. Gerdano, executive director of the American Bankruptcy Institute, said the third consecutive record year of bankruptcies correlates closely with the increased debt load carried by American families. "The same consumer spending that helps to sustain the national economy can put households at risk of needing bankruptcy relief," he added.

For Many, Spending Beats Saving

According to the Commerce Department, Americans recently set a new record for spending more than they earned.

Americans spent $100.20 for every $100 in after-tax earnings, a 0.2 percent negative savings rate. Still, enough Americans continue to show exuberance over a healthy stock market—enough so that they continue to spend beyond their means.

Commerce statistics show huge financial gaps among households, the difference between those buying into the stock market and households that cannot take advantage of the Wall Street windfall and continue to slide deeper into debt.

One investment advisor said, "There's a nasty feeling that the debt is distributed more evenly than the wealth. It's not people with the multi-million dollar stock portfolios that have the debts on their credit cards."

"I just can't stop," a Los Angeles computer programmer said, explaining why he spends more than he earns. "It's an addiction. If all the consumers keep getting more and more into debt and keep spending, nothing bad is going to happen (to the economy). So I'm doing my part."

The idea that one must save to have the financial resources necessary for retirement seems so simple. Yet saving is often given a low priority, or ignored altogether. And many individuals haven't done any planning at all.

Nearly 40 percent of baby boomers have less than $10,000 in any form of savings. Baby boomers delayed everything. They delayed entry into the work force, delayed buying homes, and delayed having children. It's no wonder they have delayed retirement planning.

Consumers Have Choices

It's not my intent to condemn consumer credit, television, advertising or other forms of media. Consumers have the ultimate decision of whether to buy or not to buy.

Consumers willfully choose to sign on the dotted line of the contract agreement or credit application. It's still an individual choice. When you decide to purchase any product you can always toss the unsigned contract back and say, "No way am I going to sign and go further into debt."

And, on the other hand, business people have the same choice to use the freedom of the American economic system to reach out and market their product. Choices and their consequences—good and bad—are mentioned throughout this book.

For those Americans who make the choice of using compound interest and show patience, becoming a financial success will be quite easy.

But the bottom line is, you're not forced to buy anything. Sure, you're coerced by a slew of sales tactics and gimmicks, but still you buy into it through cash, check or credit card. You do it of your own volition. No one put a gun to your head to make you open and empty your wallets.

Excessive spending often carries a companion called debt, which Ben Franklin warned us about two centuries ago.

Social Security Collision Course

If you're waiting for Social Security to bail you out, I have news for you. The ratio of workers to social security beneficiaries continues to decline. In 1950, there were sixteen workers per retiree. In 1960, the ratio dropped to 8.6 to 1. Today it is 3.1 to 1.

By 2011, the year the baby boomers turn sixty-five, Social Security will effectively be bankrupt because annual payroll taxes will no longer cover annual budget payments.

If our political leaders take no action, the federal government will have to raise taxes, increase debt, print more money, or reduce benefits to avoid the economic collision caused by the retirement bubble in 2011. Oh, by the way, the government just moved the retirement age up to 67; get ready for more financial tricks in the future.

The Saving Light of Compound Interest

The goal of LSA is to bring compound interest out into full light of day so everybody can have the opportunity to participate in its earnings power. I want to broadcast the might of compound interest in a loud and clear voice, not through the undertone of a small voice that only reaches a few.

Compound interest isn't a new kid on the financial block. It has been around in one form or another for thousands of years, even though you seldom hear much about it. Those who have the knowledge don't really give it much thought or consideration. In effect, they take it for granted.

Compound interest should get full recognition for being the dynamic financial driving force that it is. It should be available to everybody. It shouldn't be a shadowy, little-known secret that works its magic only for a small group of people.

Let's Save America Foundation

The Let's Save America Foundation, a companion organization to this book, is dedicated to helping all Americans understand the need to save and earn through the power of compound interest.

The Foundation plans to focus on a plan that allows school children of all grades to learn the value of saving and realize the benefits of compound interest. If you want to have a meaningful impact on children, then start teaching them about compound interest at a very early age.

If you want a world-class soccer team, you start teaching the sport at about age six. It's not hard to believe that the U.S. women's soccer team recently won the World Cup. U.S. soccer is experiencing the benefits of teaching the young. By the same token, the country is also experiencing positive results of soccer reaching critical mass.

Becoming a Winner

Michelle Akers, one of the top players in soccer history, learned early in her life that to be big, one must "think bigness." It worked for her. At 33, she was the oldest member of the 1999 world champion U.S. women's team.

> When you recognize and develop the winning qualities that you were born with, the winner you were born to be emerges.
> Anonymous

When Akers was 13, a coach told her: "Don't be afraid to go after something you desire with your whole heart, and do whatever it takes to get there."

She followed that advice and made a science of improving her game. "The best players do the basic, simple things perfectly every time and under the most pressure," she said.

Over time, Akers learned patience and didn't dwell on negatives. She followed her faith and always tried to be what she calls "a servant-leader."

"By that, I mean the leaders on our team are the ones who serve the most," she said. "They come in early and stay late; they carry luggage, pick up garbage, bag the balls, sign autographs for hours on end…whatever it takes."

Akers and soccer are good examples of critical mass. America's soccer players will get better each year. A generation of children will continue to drive the sport to a higher competitive level.

It's time for the compound interest formula to become as recognizable, and, in its own way, as valuable as reading, writing and arithmetic. People everywhere should have the choice to embrace the formula should they choose to use it.

Ignorance of the law of compound interest robs too many people through unconscious spending.

You Can Be Saved from a Life of Debt

Americans do not have to live a life of debt, and, through this book, we'll show a way out—a path with options that will lead to choices to be a saver, not a borrower.

It won't be an easy path to follow. It requires discipline, and internal tough love. You may have to dig yourself out of debt. Some people may fall by the wayside but more, many more, will make a fresh start.

By teaching the merits of compound interest, we can reach a critical mass and move the financial bell curve toward the right. When that happens, more Americans will enter the ranks of those with money. They will enjoy the advantages of financial security.

As this mass moves through Maslow's hierarchy and compound interest becomes as common as breathing, this country will enjoy the benefit of a society that has taken control of its financial destiny.

Bradley Dugdale, Jr.

LESSON I

The Compound Interest Formula: PRINCIPAL x Rate x Time = $$$

In Lesson 1, the authors discuss the initial steps to secure the success of compound interest, such as the need to save principal (money), invest wisely and let time nurture your future fortune. Also included are examples of successful models and problems to avoid on your journey to financial wealth.

The world is filled with willing people; some willing to work,
the rest willing to let them.

Robert Frost, poet

Psst, come closer, I have a secret to tell you. A clean, people-friendly secret, no X-rated or snake oil stuff. A two-word whisper that holds its own financial miracle for everyone. All that's required is that you listen, believe, buy wisely into it, and demonstrate patience.

That's it. Just a will to make an investment that earns a decent interest rate, and a show of patience. The more patience you demonstrate, the more money you earn. If you faithfully follow through, the secret could earn you a lot of money, maybe even make you wealthy.

The two-word secret I'm talking about is *compound interest*. Okay, so I tricked you, or tried to. I'll admit up front that compound interest isn't new, nor is it really a secret. Let's just say that compound interest, despite its tremendous earning capability, lives in a shadow, or a darkened closet.

Actually, this saving concept has been around for centuries. Isn't it astounding that Benjamin Franklin knew the worth of compound interest more than two hundred years ago, and many barely know of it today?

Truth is, though, that compound interest is probably as close to a sure thing as you'll find in today's financial world. Save, invest at a nice rate of return and be patient. Play the waiting game.

Keep in mind that the more you invest, the more money your investments earn. Once the strategy is in place, be cool. Sit back, relax and let it grow. Be patient and give it time; years of time. The longer the time, the larger the results.

Principal x Rate x Time

The power of compound interest is indeed incredible. When asked what was the greatest invention he'd ever seen, Albert Einstein replied without hesitation, "compound interest."

Mayer Amschel Rothschild, the German merchant who founded the greatest banking dynasty in history, once referred to the compound interest formula as "the eighth wonder of the world." Here's an example of how the formula works.

Charlie Jones, since age 18 and continuing through his working career, earns $15,000 a year working a forty-hour week (about $7.21 an hour). One day his employer offered him an opportunity to work an extra ten hours a week, and Charlie jumped at the chance.

A bachelor and junk food fanatic, Charlie would just sit around and watch television during those extra hours anyway—and the only gain he'd realize would be his weight. So he signed on to work the extra ten hours a week through age forty before going back to his usual forty-hour work week.

But then an idea leaped out in his mind. Instead of frittering away the extra money he'd earn, he'd dump every penny of it into a savings program and forget about it. He wouldn't touch it; not for a house, a car, or trips to other countries. He'd hold it as a retirement plum.

> We must use time as a tool, not as a couch.
> President John F. Kennedy

Let's assume that for twenty-three years he worked the extra ten hours a week and that after paying state and federal taxes, Social Security and such, he saved the rest of the additional income of about $3.60 an hour.

True to his idea, the years flew by and he never, not even once, checked on the total worth of his account, which had chugged along earning 8 percent each year.

At age 65, Charlie finally checked his account and almost keeled over. It had grown to $833,934.17 at the 8 percent appreciation rate. Wow, imagine that! By working an extra ten hours a week and following the compound interest formula, the results produced $833,934.17.

After splashing his face with cold water, Charlie quickly got on the phone and called his financial advisor, who whipped out his trusty calculator and started running figures.

> The greatest things ever done on earth have been done little by little.
> William Jennings Bryan

Charlie, his advisor exclaimed, if your money had earned at the 10 percent rate, your net worth would be $1,814,202.89. Furthermore, if Charlie would wait until age seventy, using the same 10 percent appreciation rate, his net worth would be $2,984,924.23—a hop, skip and jump to nearly $3 million.

What happened? Charlie inquired of his financial guru. How did this come about?

Simple, his advisor said in a prideful voice. "The miracle of compound interest." The miracle created wealth beyond Charlie's wildest dreams.

"By pitching in all the money you earned for working extra hours, you helped supercharge your compounding. You correctly followed the compound interest formula and let it work."

In other words, the longer Charlie left his investment untouched and let it compound, the more money he earned. That's all it takes. Nothing to feed, water or take for a walk. No sweat, no problem.

"You made a bundle, my friend," the advisor said.

There are thousands of riveting stories to be told, some more spectacular than Charlie's. But society glamorizes people who suddenly become rich by winning lotteries, signing fat movie deals or sports contracts, and, in some cases, through inheritance.

Charlie, after all, earned his through a simple way that works for anyone who uses the formula. He worked, and unfailingly invested part of his earnings for twenty-three years.

Some of the suddenly rich are able to emotionally handle their newly found wealth. Then there are others who obtain wealth and lead miserable, self-destructive lives because they're emotionally unprepared to cope with such good fortune. Life holds out to everyone a series of opportunities.

America is the epitome of opportunity, choice and tradeoffs. If you believe, and really want a better life—a life that includes a higher degree of financial stability for you and your family—it's there for the taking. It's up to you to reach out and grab it.

People can chart their own destination to whatever level of financial stability they wish by using compound interest. All that's needed is to save early, invest wisely and stick with it through the long haul. Once a saving program starts, the investor must be strong enough to resist the spending temptation of the moment and leave the principal in the formula to grow.

Compound interest is a financial law. The law is working constantly. The formula either works for you or against you. It doesn't care. The formula can produce financial abundance or financial servitude. If you choose to abuse credit and accumulate excessive debt, you'll drown in a financial rushing stream of interest payments.

Your lending institutions—banks, credit unions, or pawnshops—also understand and use the concept of compound interest and will do so to their advantage.

The ten chapters of this book will teach common sense financial tactics that produce financial freedom. If you choose to use them, you'll be on the path to financial success. If you wait or ignore compound interest your choices will constantly diminish.

The secret to having maximum control over how you live is to be able to get by comfortably on spending less than you earn. Spend less, save, and invest.

If you don't obtain some money (principal)—and it needn't be hundreds or thousands of dollars—the financial formula won't work.

In life, we make a decision—either consciously or unconsciously—about our financial habits. Inevitably, we become one or the other; a spender, a borrower or a saver.

If you can't use discipline and save a few bucks a month, you have nothing to invest. If you have nothing to plant, you have nothing to grow. Compound interest will not and can not work for you.

Let's look at the three options that face an American consumer. Consumers have a choice to spend, borrow, or save.

The Spender

If a spender earns and then spends $1,000 each month, saving not a penny of principal for forty years, how much will the spender accumulate? Nothing. The spender failed to save any money to invest.

IF A SPENDER		
Earns per month	$	1,000
Spends per month	-$	1,000
Saves nothing		0

Always taking out of the pot, and never putting in, one soon comes to the bottom.
Benjamin Franklin

There's an old song that goes, "nothin' from nothin' leaves nothin." That old melodic refrain says it all. If you spend down to nothing, it leaves you with nothing. Zero multiplied by any number equals zero.

Zero x Rate x Time = Zero

A little "seed money" is necessary to start the compound interest motor running. As an old hair-care commercial of past decades used to tell us, "a little dab'll do 'ya." A small amount of principal will get you started.

But equally appropriate is the old declaration, "the more, the merrier." Applying this utterance to the compound interest formula, the more money you put in your earnings account along the way, the merrier you'll be years later when you see the growth of your investment.

The Borrower

For borrowers, however, the story is quite different. A borrower makes $1,000 a month and spends $1,200 a month, going $200 in debt each month. The monthly deficit left alone for 40 years equals…problems. Compound interest obviously works against you here. Bummer!

IF A BORROWER		
Earns per month	$	1,000
Spends per month	-$	1,200
Owes per month	-$	<200>

Allowed to continue, this pattern of behavior has disastrous consequences. A monthly debt of $200 adds up to a yearly debt of more than $2,400, including charged interest. Suddenly, the complexion of the smaller monthly debt looms taller and more intimidating, doesn't it?

Years of overspending has a price, and for more than a million people every year, that price is bankruptcy. The way to wealth is straightforward and simple; spend less than you earn, avoid debt, then save and invest wisely for growth. It greatly helps if you want wealth. Once you establish the want, you must control your spending habits to attain it.

> Do not accustom yourself to consider debt only as an inconvenience; you will find it a calamity.
> Samuel Johnson, critic and lexicographer

The Saver

A saver earns $1,000 a month and spends only $900. He takes the $100 left over each month and invests it at an earnings rate of 12 percent a year, and compounds it for forty years.

IF A SAVER		
Earns per month	**$**	**1,000**
Spends per month	**$**	**900**
Saves per month	**$**	**100**

If a saver invests $100 a month and it grows at a 12 percent earnings rate for forty years, the power of compound interest will increase it to a total of $1,176,477.25. The saver made the formula work to his or her benefit. The saver took the monthly principal of $100 and faithfully invested it at a yearly rate of 12 percent and let it grow for a time of forty years. A textbook example of how compound interest works.

Here's another good example of how small amounts of money can grow huge through the wonder of compound interest. A 25-year-old investing $25 a month in stocks that consistently returns 10.2 percent builds up more than $168,042.36 by age sixty-five. Think about it! Just $25 a month; the price of a sweatshirt, or a dinner for two.

How The Rich Become Poor

The faster you spend, the bigger the problem becomes, and even the mega wealthy aren't immune.

A well known singer makes and spends a lot of money. He buys homes, jewels and big, expensive cars as fast as he trots out smash hits. His fortune has been estimated at $256 million, and from 1991 to 1996 alone his income reached $131 million. He's had at least one song on the charts every year since 1971. The man can sing.

The musician is apparently a far better singer than he is a financier. He recently shopped around for a $40 million loan to help pay some of his considerable debts. To get the loan, he will give up proceeds from old and future hit songs, it was reported. People in debt have no choice. Like it or not they often have to borrow today in order to pay for yesterday.

The same report noted that the singer spends up to $400,000 a week on credit cards.

Most of the loan money will be used to pay off debts in the United States and Britain including an alleged $11 million overdraft with an English bank, and a loan near $4 million.

> When prosperity comes,
> do not use all of it.
> Confucius, philosopher

Let's not pass judgment on the singer, because he's only one of millions who spend more than they earn and then need a bill consolidation loan to make financial ends meet. In all fairness, it should be noted that the singer isn't broke. Far from it, as a matter of fact. It's just that he has no ready cash, a commodity he needs to pay his bills. Creditors, after all, are not noted for their patience, especially around payment time.

Excessive spending has a price and many times it leads to financial chaos. It happens all too often to those in the arts and entertainment industry; to highly paid sports figures, to financial wizards who make a bad call or a wrong move, and even to the rich who inherited their fortunes.

They are the ones who get the media attention and wind up on the front pages of newspapers or become the lead stories for television news programs.

It's a rare day when the media points out the goodness that comes from the simple formula that works every time. For much of the media, it has to be bad to be good.

> Only 19 percent of American
> millionaires receive any wealth
> of any kind from a
> trust or an estate.
> The Millionaire Next Door

False affluence (keeping up with the Joneses) invades the financial territory of many Americans throughout all economic levels. It strikes the big and the little, the rich and poor and the in-between. If not you, then your neighbor next door or a block away—stressed out because their paycheck can't cover the bills.

Is there a way out of this mess? Certainly! We're not talking rocket science here, but it will require financial discipline and changes in spending or earning habits. This book is about financial common sense. Let's ask a question.

Which of the three—the spender, the saver, or the borrower—has less stress in their lives? A no-brainer, huh? Of course, the saver has less stress than do the others. The saver knows he's planned ahead and will have a comfortable retirement life. Not so for the spender or the borrower, who failed to put away any funds for their golden years.

Financial wealth for all of us starts with this premise: spend less than you earn. Then save and invest wisely over a long period of time, thus allowing compound interest to work its magic.

Summary

- Be a saver, not a spender or borrower.
- Be bold enough to invest at a decent interest rate of return, then show patience.
- Take on a second job if that's the only way you can save principal.
- Once in a savings program, leave the money intact so it can benefit from compound interest.

LESSON II

How to Get Principal:
Use the Law of Compensation

We can't save and enjoy watching our money grow through the formula of compound interest if we're flat broke and deep in debt. This lesson talks about these issues and offer sound alternatives to help us make ourselves more marketable in the ever-changing job market.

When I am asked by the young people for
the secret of success, I try to make them
understand that there is no mystery about
it, that the answer is summed up in two words—
hard work.

James Cash Penney, retailer

Obtaining principal (money) to plug into the compound interest formula is critical to long term financial success. There are three ways to obtain principal. Spend less than you earn obviously is one option. Another is to increase your income by working smarter or longer, like Charlie did in Lesson I. And the third way is to enhance your knowledge through education.

Let's first discuss working smarter and longer, and using the law of compensation.

The law of compensation is a strategy to increase your income at your present job. The law of compensation has several components; do more than is expected, increase productivity, never burn a bridge and read to stay current. The more income one earns, the greater the investment principal that can be channeled into the compound interest formula.

If you use the law of compensation, you will not need to make a dramatic change in your work habits to have a meaningful impact on the financial choices. Often you can improve your current financial situation at your existing job with no cost to you or your employer. This law only asks that you reallocate your time and use it wisely. A simple change in attitude and increased productivity can produce dramatic results.

Charlie Jones decided to work an extra ten hours a week and invested the income for twenty-three years. It yielded him $833,934.17. If Charlie had used the law of compensation, who knows how much he would have accumulated?

Do More Than Is Expected

Let's analyze the activities Bell curve.

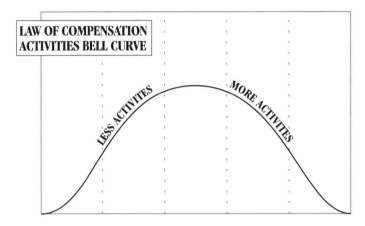

LEVEL OF ACTIVITIES PER EMPLOYEES

If, as the employer, you observed all of the workers, which one would most likely get a raise? Which employee would you promote as manager? Which employee is more likely to get fired? It's common sense, isn't it?

If, as an employee, you decide to arrive early and leave late, and do more activities than the other workers, what do you think would happen?

Here's what happened for industrialist Andrew Carnegie. At age 14, Carnegie viewed his messenger job at Western Union as an opportunity to move up. He had a solid plan, too: catch the eye of his boss by doing more than expected.

He started by memorizing names, faces and addresses of people to whom he made frequent deliveries. Before long he recognized them on the street, and thus, cut his delivery time. After teaching himself to operate the telegraph, his boss promoted him to telegraph operator.

"The battle of life is already half won by the young man who is brought personally in contact with high officials," Carnegie noted. "Everybody should do something beyond the sphere of his duties—something (that) attracts the attention of those over him."

Not everyone will experience Carnegie's success, but everyone can copy his plan.

Carnegie went on to found Carnegie Steel Co. and become one of the richest men in the world.

Increase the Productivity or Bottom Line of the Business

Businesses survive because of profits. Without profits, there are no jobs.

My first full-time job was in the fast food industry making tacos. One of my chores was to prepare and grind the lettuce—a two-hour

> Make every decision as if you owned the whole company.
> Robert Townsend, former president, Avis car rentals

job as a new employee. Before long, my best friend and I started a friendly contest to see which of us could complete the task quicker. Within a week, we had cut our time in half. Within two weeks the time was down to a mere thirty minutes. It became a challenge to see who could work the fastest. Before long, we finished below twenty-five minutes. A new standard of productivity was established and both the employer and employees benefited.

If you help bring more money to the business and you're doing the most activities, you'll greatly improve your chances to be first in line to share in the company's good fortune.

Never Burn an Employment Bridge

It's easier to find a job if you have one at the time you're job-searching. Make yourself so valuable that if you leave for another job, the boss will fret over how he or she will replace you. Then if you ever need a job,

> Everything comes to him who hustles while he waits.
> Thomas Edison, inventor

your old employer would hire you back in an instant. They'll remember the extra effort you put forth for the company.

Read and Stay Current

When I graduated from college I thought I was through with tests, studying and reading. Wrong! I've taken more tests after college than I ever did in school.

It's important to stay current with what's going on in your industry. If you don't, you'll get recycled and become obsolete in the market place.

Let's put it another way: if you needed a life threatening operation, which doctor would you choose? The one that never stops learning, reads all the current medical books, journals and periodicals, takes classes and is on top of his profession? Or the one that hadn't picked up a medical journal in 10 years?

The man who graduates today and stops learning tomorrow is uneducated the day after.
Newton D. Baker, lawyer and public official

Reading is an inexpensive way to make a dramatic impact on your income.

Readers are Leaders

Two great American Presidents—George Washington and Abraham Lincoln—and India's Mohandas Gandhi, were avid readers throughout their lives. They utilized their ability to read to the fullest extent.

Gandhi, a college dropout, passed the barrister examination in England and became a timid and self-conscious lawyer in his younger years. Realizing his weakness, Gandhi used reading as a tool to conquer his fright and to improve his barrister skills.

He knew he was afraid because he lacked confidence. In order to gain confidence, Gandhi delved into law studies until he felt completely comfortable with its practice. Armed with this knowledge, he soon became able to successfully mediate between parties.

Gandhi eventually gave up his law practice and championed the movement of love and nonviolent resistance.

President Lincoln read everything he could get his hands on. Young Lincoln read the book, The Life of George Washington, by Mason Locke Weems, until he could quote whole paragraphs. He was inspired as he read about Washington's battles for liberty.

The Bible also moved Lincoln. He read it many times, copying whole passages of Scripture on paper with a charcoal pencil so he could memorize them. At night, he'd hit the law books, and in 1836 he passed the bar and began practicing law in Springfield, Ill.

Lincoln pushed himself to become more informed, acute and decisive. He was patient, and kept faith that he was headed to the top.

President Washington's formal education lasted only a few years. Though not a scholar like Thomas Jefferson, Washington still read widely throughout his life. He loved classical drama, and often used the theatrics he'd read about to persuade men to follow him in both the military and political arenas.

"There was a powerful drive in this big young man to better himself," historian Paul Johnson wrote in his book, A History of the American People. "He developed a good, neat, legible hand. To improve his manners, he copied out 110 maxims, originally compiled by a French Jesuit as instructions for young aristocrats."

The Mark Victor Hansen Challenge

Mark Victor Hansen, the author of Chicken Soup for the Soul, was in Coeur d'Alene, Idaho, in the fall of 1989. At that time, Mark told me that if I read thirty minutes a day about my industry, or self-improvement, I would double my income.

What a challenge! If that's all it takes to double one's income, I could do that. Being an over-achiever, if a half-hour would double my income, what would an hour do? I decided to read an hour a day before I went to work.

Living in the Pacific Time Zone, the New York Stock Exchange starts trading here at 6:30 a.m. So I set my alarm clock at 4:45 a.m. to get my reading completed before leaving for work.

I must admit that the first week was quite a challenge, but I hung in there (thank goodness for caffeine). The uninterrupted time was remarkable. I devoured books. It was amazing. I went from reading one or two books a year to between forty and fifty. The energy and excitement I generated is hard to explain.

I found myself speeding to get to work. There was so much to learn. I came up with more ideas than I could implement. The bottom line is that not only did I double my income in two years, it doubled again in the following two years.

Other than the time (which I would have spent watching television or sleeping) it didn't cost anything. If you can't afford the books, America has the best public library system in the world—thanks to Benjamin Franklin. There are plenty of libraries around—and they're free. Give the Mark Victor Hansen challenge a chance. What do you have to lose?

An investment in knowledge pays the best interest.
Ben Franklin

Supercharge the Law of Compensation by Modeling

One of the fastest ways to learn is through modeling. Modeling is observing the activities of other successful people and repeating everything they do.

I fought the system during my first six years in the investment profession. I thought I was smarter than anyone who had ever been in the business. My first response was to complain about the company, my manager, and the marketplace. Everyone was at fault except me. You name it and I'd blame it.

I eventually transferred to another office, hoping that would change my luck. My new manager was the most successful person in our company at that time.

My fortunes changed a little but I was still complaining and looking for the fountain of success. I complained to my new manager, who was so busy that he didn't have time to listen. He was always polite, and would have me wait while he did business right before my eyes. I usually left his office without engaging in conversation.

Then it struck me. He was successful because he did more activities than anyone else in the firm. He was the activities king.

> I pay less attention to what men say; I just watch what they do.
> Andrew Carnegie, industrialist

I started to observe his behavior. Then I started to mimic his behavior and low and behold, my activities increased, my production rose and so did my income.

By modeling a successful person's behavior I was able to produce similar results. You don't need to reinvent the wheel to become successful. Just correctly use a wheel that already cruises smoothly down the road.

If you choose to use the law of compensation to increase your income through increased activities, never burning a bridge, reading or modeling, you will be amazed by the positive results. The world is loaded with examples of people who started with low-paying jobs; some in the mailrooms, or digging ditches, or flipping burgers—many with no money or education. Still, they hung in there and pursued their dreams. Some became so successful that they built their own financial empires and helped change the world.

> There's always a way to get ahead if you're determined and creative. It's tempting to blame circumstances for your problems, but it's a waste of time. Instead, reach inside yourself. You'll come up with ways to cope and take pride in meeting the challenge.
> Glen Bell, restauranteur

What do you have to lose? What do you have to gain?

Education Pays Off In Many Ways

Another way to obtain principal is through enhancing your education. Education increases your value to an employer. Education shows that you can set and accomplish goals.

> The direction in which education starts a man will determine his future life.
> Plato, Greek philosopher

The benefits of a good education are enormous and have been laboriously expounded upon for decades, even centuries. The oft-used truism, "you can never have too much education," is truer now than ever before.

A college education is essential in today's competitive workplace. Many professions now require an education beyond a four-year college degree. A high school diploma today will not give you that competitive edge in tomorrow's job market.

Even a four-year university degree doesn't guarantee you a job now; it only allows you an equal opportunity to compete. From that point on, it's up to you to get the job and to protect it.

> One is not born a genius; one becomes a genius.
> Simone de Beauvoir, writer

How Education Adds to Your Income

Education	Median Household Income (1996)
Less than 9th grade	$20,781
9th to 12th (no diploma)	$24,575
High school graduate	$38,563
Some college (no degree)	$44,814
Associate degree	$51,176
Bachelor's degree	$64,293
Master's degree	$76,065
Professional degree	$102,557
Doctorate degree	$92,316

Figure that the take-home, or after-tax, difference in earning between the high school graduate and the dropout is $8,000 a year at age eighteen.

Then, let's figure that the difference in take-home pay is invested each year from ages eighteen to sixty-seven in assets that earn 8 percent each year.

Would you believe that the high school graduate's net worth would be $4,874,928 more than it would be if he had dropped out of high school?

It's probably unreasonable to assume high school graduates will spend no more than high school dropouts earn, and invest the difference. Much of the advantage of the extra income comes from the joy of spending it before retirement.

But that means the benefit of the extra education is actually greater than the $4,874,928 at retirement. It means if retirement wealth is what a high school student values most, he or she can have it.

It's not a good idea, however, to think of education entirely in terms of the financial advantages. Certainly there are other advantages of obtaining an education.

A good education can provide intellectual satisfactions that no amount of money can buy.

Edwin "Buzz" Aldrin Jr., the second man to walk on the moon, knew the benefits of a good education. He focused on learning at an early age and never stopped his studies.

The Apollo 11 rocket with a crew of Aldrin, Neil Armstrong and Mike Collins blasted off to the moon on July 16, 1969. Aldrin helped steer the 240,000-mile flight that landed on the moon July 20, when he followed Armstrong out of the space capsule, and the pair became the first human beings to step on the lunar surface.

Aldrin graduated from the U.S. Military Academy in West Point, N.Y. in 1951. He earned a Ph.D in astronautics from Massachusetts Institute of Technology in 1962. Even as a youth, Aldrin realized he needed to learn how to conduct himself in any situation.

He also knew he needed excellent grades to overcome the stiff competition for flight training school. He studied and read constantly, all the while staying focused on academics. It worked. He graduated third highest in his class in 1951.

Aldrin used education to increase his choices in life. Education not only increased his income, it also let him pursue a life passion.

The first component of the compound interest formula is principal (money). If you don't have principal the formula won't work. Zero X rate X time=zero. You can only obtain principal by spending less than you earn. The use of the law of compensation or enhancing one's education will accelerate the amount of principal that can be used in the formula.

This book is about using common sense to obtain financial security. It should not be construed that money is the answer to everything. It is not. But it does increase the number of choices you have in your life.

If you've decided to save some (principal) investment money, read Lesson III for an explanation of how to make your money grow. Rate of return is the next component of compound interest.

Summary

- Become ingenious in saving money. Cut down expenses.
- Try to make more money in your present job through increased productivity and promotions.
- Increase activities such as reading in your profession. Stay current.
- Reallocate your time and use it wisely.
- Keep a positive attitude.
- Find at least one person you can use as a role model.
- Increase your education. It will help in the workplace and also give you intellectual satisfaction.

LESSON III

Principal x **RATE** x Time = $$$

With Money in Hand,
Where's the Best Place to Put it?

Once we save a little money, what do we do with it? Feeling insecure about our investment skills? We don't want to lose what we worked so hard to save. Worry not, the authors give us a clear path to success through a variety of investment vehicles, and even sound warnings to potential potholes that could slow our financial progress.

Nobody can really guarantee the future. The best we can do is size up the chances, calculate the risks involved, estimate our ability to deal with them and then make our plans with confidence.

Henry Ford II, auto executive

Principal x Rate x Time = $

The next component of the formula is rate of return. Now that you have principal, where are you going to invest it? The decision on where to invest your money (principal) has a dramatic impact on the result.

As in Lesson 1, any number multiplied by zero still equals zero. This mathematical fact eliminates the option of stuffing your principal into a coffee can, putting it under a mattress or burying it in a hole in the back yard.

Loaner or Owner

There are two general types of investments; fixed income and ownership (stocks or equity).

Fixed income is when you lend your money to a bank (savings accounts, certificates of deposit), or to the U. S. government (treasury bills, notes or bonds) for a set period of time and at a fixed rate of return.

Generally with fixed income, the longer you lend your money the higher the rate of return earned on the investment. The comforting thing about lending your money to a bank or the government is that the principal is guaranteed, and the investment has a set maturity.

But you'll pay the price for the comfort of a guaranteed interest rate, and that price is a lower rate of return. The average rate of return from 1925 through 1998 on short-term government T-bills is 3.9 percent. The return on long term government bonds is 5.2 percent over the same period of time.

Equities, which mean ownership through stock or equity mutual funds, are another place to invest your money. Since 1925, ownership through the common stock has produced an 11.2 percent return. That's twice as much as bonds and almost triple the rate of T-bills.

With equities, there are no guarantees, the principal invested fluctuates up and down in value. Your investment is now subject to the business cycle expansions and contractions, and to the emotions of fear and greed as your money expands and contracts in value.

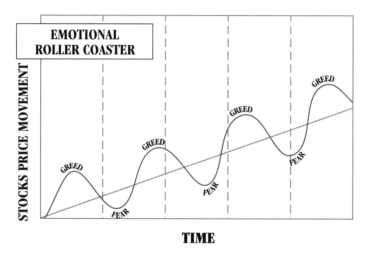

If you have the proper temperament for ownership through equities, it is one of the best and easiest methods to financial success using compound interest.

There are no gains without pains.
Benjamin Franklin

It's important to remember that stocks occasionally decline in price. If you invest in stocks, you must be ready to accept both the increases and the decreases. There's no free lunch.

However, stocks are resilient, having over the years survived through wars, periods of inflation, recessions, depressions, nuclear bombings, presidential assassinations and a multitude of other trials and tribulations—even Y2K.

Most corporations have the ability to adjust to almost any business climate. The way to reduce risk with equities is time and diversification. Historically, the longer you own equities the lower the risk and the more successful your investment outcome.

A 1998 report by a leading mutual fund company noted that American stocks did not have a negative return in any ten-year period between 1948 and 1997.

All the investment experts will tell you is that the power of time increases your probability of reaching the historical rates of return. History also shows that the longer you hold stocks, the more likely your chances for beating the investment returns of T-bills, bonds and inflation.

Stocks are the Best Choice for Long Term

Average Total Return 1948-1997 (50 years)		
Stocks	**Bonds**	**Cash**
13.1%	**6.1%**	**5.0%**

Over the last fifty years, if your investment strategy was long-term (at least ten years in length), stocks have easily outperformed bonds and cash.

Stocks are always more volatile over shorter periods than either bonds or fixed interest investments. But the longer the stock investment time frame the less risk you have of losing money. It logically follows, then, that the longer you have to reach your financial goal, the more stock ownership becomes important.

Let's analyze the results from 1925 to 1998, including the 1929 stock market crash. Look at the illustration below.

S&P 500
December 31, 1925 to December 31, 1998

Holding Periods (Years)	Up Periods	Down Periods	% of Up Periods
1	53	20	73
5	62	7	90
10	62	2	97
15	59	0	100

If you held equities for one year holding periods the chance of a positive return was 73 percent. Five-year periods were 90 percent. Ten-year periods were 97 percent and 15-year holding periods 100 percent.

Reviewing the last fifty years, the results get even better.

Over a one-year holding period, 80 percent of American stocks had positive results during the forty-nine year period. For a five-year holding period, the positive return increased to 96 percent. A ten-year holding period resulted in a 100 percent positive return. But remember, these performances are after-the-fact (historical) and do not guarantee future results.

Percent of Time Stocks Have Had Positive Results

1948-1997		Holding Period
80%	Positive Return	1 year
96%	Positive Return	5 years
100%	Positive Return	10 years

The longer you hold equities the better the chance of not losing principal and earning the historical investment return.

Volatility isn't the only risk to investing principal. The greatest threat to any investor is inflation.

Beware of the Inflation Train

As discussed earlier, when you lend money your principal in a fixed income instrument, you can expect a lower rate of return. The longer you lend money, the higher the rate of return. Keep in mind that while most fixed income is guaranteed and may be safe havens for short-term savings, they are not considered good long-term investments because inflation slowly erodes their purchasing power.

Many people place their savings in low-earning treasury bills and certificates of deposit because they fear losing money from the volatility of stocks or other equity investments.

Many fixed income investors are going broke safely after paying taxes and adjusting the returns for inflation. Short-term interest rates normally hover slightly above the inflation rate. When you report the interest income on your taxes, you barely keep pace with inflation.

Going Broke Safely

Short-term fixed income:

$ 10,000			
	x	3.90%	historic short-term rate of return
$ 390			interest
	x	25%	tax bracket
$ - 97.50		tax	
$ 292.50			after tax return
$ -310.00		3.10%	historical inflation rate
<$ 17.50>			after tax, after inflation return
			negative .175%

Long-term fixed income:

$ 10,000			
	x	5.2%	historic short-term rate of return
$ 520			interest
	x	25%	tax bracket
$ - 130		tax	
$ 390			after tax return
$ - 310		3.10%	historical inflation rate
+$ 80			after tax, after inflation return
			positive .8%

Equities:

$ 10,000			
	x	11.2%	historic short-term rate of return
$ 1,120			
	x	25%	tax bracket
$ - 280		tax	
$ 840			after tax return
$ - 310		3.10%	historical inflation rate
+$ 530			after tax, after inflation return
			positive 5.30%

I used a 25 percent tax rate to keep the examples consistent. If investors hold stocks longer than a year, they qualify for a preferential tax rate called capital gain. This drops the tax rate substantially below the ordinary income tax charged for fixed income investments.

The average annual rate of inflation has been 3.1 percent since 1925. Over the last fifty years (1948-1998) the rate has averaged 3.91 percent.

The purchasing power of $100 has dipped 85 percent in the last fifty years to $14.69. Here's what it takes to buy today what you bought twenty-five years ago.

	1974	1999	% Increase
Consumer Price Index	$ 100	$ 355	
Postage Stamp[1]	$ .10	$ .33	230
The Wall Street Journal[2]	$ .20	$ .75	275
Cadillac Sedan de Ville[3]	$ 8,000	$ 39,000	391
University of Texas tuition[4]	$ 3,480	$ 8,872	154
Super Bowl Ticket, box seats[5]	$ 15	$ 325	2066

Source: U.S. Postal Service, The Wall Street Journal, General Motors, University of Texas, The National Football League

[1] Price of first-class stamp

[2] Newsstand price

[3] Manufacturer's suggested retail price

[4] One year out-of-state tuition for academic years 1973-74 and 1998-99

[5] Box seats face value

Money needed in future to equal $100 today, based at a 4 percent inflation rate.

Today	Years	4% Inflation
$100	5	$ 122
	10	$ 148
	15	$ 180
	20	$ 219
	25	$267

Source: Towers Data Systems, HYPO. A 4% annual inflation rate is assumed. Based on the annual average inflation rate of 3.91% from December 31, 1948 to December 31, 1998.

If you have a long term financial goal, it is hard to reach it using bonds or certificates of deposit. It's tough to beat inflation long-term if you invest in bonds or certificates of deposit (CDs).

The question is not if you can afford to invest in stocks, but whether you can afford to bypass them. Equities are the most accessible, liquid, investor-friendly security that outpaces inflation over the long haul.

The table below shows various rates of return necessary to stay ahead of inflation at selected tax rates.

Maintaining Purchase Power
Required Minimum Return

Tax Rate	Inflation Rate				
	3%	4%	5%	6%	7%
28%	4.2	5.5	6.9	8.3	9.7
31%	4.3	5.8	7.2	8.7	10.1
36%	4.7	6.3	7.8	9.4	10.9
40%	5.0	6.7	8.3	10.0	11.7
45%	5.5	7.3	9.1	10.9	12.7
50%	6.0	8.0	10.0	12.0	14.0

Years ago, I met a school teacher who had diligently set aside at least $50 a month. A conservative person, she invested in U.S. savings bonds and certificates of deposit. She invested faithfully each month for over forty-five years.

For most of those years, her savings earned 3 to 5 percent rate of return until fixed income interest rates increased in the early 1980s. She had held some of her U.S. savings bonds over forty years. Many of the bonds lay dormant, drawing no interest.

Still, by the time I met her, her savings had accumulated to more than $600,000. How had this happened?

The teacher had successfully used two components—principal and time—of the compound interest formula. She used thrift by saving each month (principal). Then she used time, by investing a steady amount every month over forty-five years.

> A little knowledge that acts is worth infinitely more than much knowledge that is idle.
> Khalil Gibran, writer

The missing element of the formula for most of her forty-five years was rate of return. Had she invested her money in equities for the entire time, her value would have grown into millions. Still, not bad for a school teacher saving a little principal each month.

Summary

- Be an owner, not a loaner.
- Banks, governments usually offer lower interest rates for guaranteed return on principal.
- Stocks, mutual funds offer no guarantee, and money fluctuates in value, but since 1925 have averaged a yearly 11.2 rate of return.
- Equities (same as stocks) is one of the best ways to use compound interest.

LESSON IV

Principal x Rate x TIME
Time: It's Ours to Use or Lose

The authors use examples to explain the importance of how time affects the growth of financial investments. They also let us know through words and graphs how to calculate the amount of years it takes for an investment's value to double by using the Rule of 72.

Success is more a function of consistent
common sense than it is of a genius.
Anonymous

Now you have principal and you know about rate of return. Time, the third element of the equation, is the magical part of the formula of compound interest. The longer you leave your principal in the formula, the more it grows. The most difficult obstacle to investment success is patience and discipline.

We live in an impatient society—instant breakfast, microwave ovens, eat on the run—go, go, go. Whatever it is we want, we want it fast and we want it now. We abhor the thought of having to wait for anything. It's the time part (waiting) that makes it difficult for many Americans to execute the patience required in the formula of compound interest.

The time component of compound interest has an inherent element of common sense. Stephen Covey, author of the book "Seven Habits of Highly Successful People," describes a concept that success in any venture is like farming. You must first plant your seed (principal) in fertile ground (rate) and then let it grow (time). If nurtured, it will grow at a consistent and natural pace. You can't force farming. Compound interest works the same way.

If you plant an apple seed, you can't harvest apples when the plant first pops out of the ground. You need to nurture and fertilize the plant and be patient. Over time, as the tree matures, it will produce a bountiful harvest of apples year after year for generations to come.

Investment wealth is accumulated step by step; like farming, it can't be rushed. It reminds me of the fable, The Tortoise and the Hare.

Talking to friends within deliberate hearing distance of the tortoise, the agile and quick-witted hare said derisively, "Look at that tortoise, what a dull plodder. Always looking straight ahead, neither to the right or left. He drags along through the mud eating old, burnt grass and dirty roots as he comes to them, covering no more territory in a day's time than I can rack up in two or three effortless bounds."

The tortoise blushed upon hearing the hare's self-serving remarks and spoke up in his own defense. "Mouth on, harebrain," he snapped with sleepy eyes between munches on a piece of straw sticking out one side of his mouth. "I have neither your swiftness nor your well-formed legs, but I challenge you to an investment race."

"Done," said the hare, with bluster. "I'm gonna leave footmarks all over your back." They agreed to a goal and started together.

The tortoise jogged along on his hindquarters at his same, plodding rate and it wasn't long before the hare left him behind and out of sight.

Shortly thereafter the hare grew impatient. He decided to try another investment idea he had heard at work. Well, that idea worked for a few days until he read of something else in a newsletter which promised boundless riches in a short period of time.

The rabbit jumped from idea to idea, always looking for the quick return. He had plenty of time to beat the boring tortoise.

Try as he might, the rabbit continued hopping from idea to idea to idea. He finally tired and sat down beside the road, never coming close to the finish line that the tortoise had already crossed.

Always looking for the fast way to success, most investment rabbits get hit by cars. They fall prey to lotteries or investment traps or scams.

A recently conducted survey pointed out that 25 percent of Americans believe their best chance to get rich is by playing the lottery, not saving and investing. People living paycheck to paycheck are more likely to feel that way. Ignorance of how small amounts of money can grow keeps millions of people from realizing their financial potential.

> A man with the average mentality but with control, a definite goal...and above all with the power of application and labor, wins in the end.
> President William Howard Taft

Making good use of time is undoubtedly one of life's most important decisions. Let's look at how four astute turtles used compound interest.

Take the cases of Jake, 19, and his younger siblings, Jim, 14, and 8-year-old twins, Dealer and Bess. All were thrifty and competitive and put most every penny they earned into equity investments.

At age 19, Jake invested $2,000 and did so each following year until he reached the age of 25. Then he stopped. Never put in another red cent. The day after his 25th birthday, Jake, a rambling man, walked down the road and just disappeared. He circled the world a time or two and then one day, right after his 65th birthday, he showed up at home, ambling up the same dusty road that he took to get out of town those many years ago.

He didn't waste any time before checking on the value of his account and found his initial investment of $14,000 had grown to $929,177, compounding at a yearly average rate of 10.2 percent. His money had increased 66-fold. The magic of compound interest worked for Jake.

He stuck around town a short while and got reacquainted with his sister Bess, then announced, "I feel the need to ramble, but now I can ramble in style." Jake converted his principal into some monthly cash flow and left the next day.

Jim started his own account at age 14 and pitched in $2,000 yearly through age 18, a total of five years ($10,000). Like his brother Jake, he stopped further contributions. He also stopped going to school, bailing out after his senior year of high school.

Quite athletic, Jim soon caught the attention of a traveling circus owner and joined up as a flying trapeze man. He wintered with the circus in south central Oklahoma and toured through the rest of America for most of his life.

Jim's career with the circus and his life as a performer on the trapeze ended the day he slipped away from his "catcher" and busted a leg. So, nearing age 65, he limped home and checked on his account. Well, his $10,000 contribution now was worth $1,172,891. He danced a jig on his one good leg, he was so happy. His money had multiplied 117-fold.

"I'm going back to the circus," he said happily to Bess. "This time, I'll be the owner, and I can use the trapeze as much as I want." He left the next day.

The last boy, Dealer, and Bess, his twin sister, had watched and taken notice of their two brothers when they opened their investment accounts. So it was only natural that on their eighth birthday they paid a visit to an investment advisor, who helped them set up individual saving plans.

Dealer opened his with $500, and on each of the following five birthdays upped the ante to $750, $1,000, $1,250, $1,500 and $1,750. Then he ceased contributing to his account.

Bess placed $500 in her account, and then in successive years contributed $750; 1,000; $1,250; $1,500 and $1,750. But, from her 14th to her 65 birthday, the rubber hit the road. From that point on, she each year contributed $2,000. She was always a quick study.

Dealer, meanwhile, wanted to be a writer so he left after graduating from high school and went to live in France, somewhere on the Left Bank of the Seine in Paris. He didn't earn much money from his writing but as the years passed he learned to enjoy the pleasures of the city.

Finally, downtrodden and worn out over receiving so many rejection slips from book publishers, he returned home just after his 65th birthday to check on his account. To his surprise, his $6,750 investment came to $1,611,077.92. His initial investment had compounded an average of 10 percent over the years. The $6,750 had grown 239 times. Instantly, he decided to leave for France the next day.

After a couple gasps of air, he hurried to a nearby church where Bess, having become a nun after graduating from a known school of religion, spent most of her waking hours.

> There is no royal road to anything. One thing at a time, and all things in succession. That which grows slowly endures.
> Josiah G. Holland,
> newspaper and magazine editor

He told her of his newfound wealth and it piqued her interest. She hadn't checked her account in years and years but she knew it had done well. She'd been helping others and hadn't had time to hardly even think about it.

In Dealer's presence, Bess picked up the church phone and under the intense eyes of her brother, dialed her financial advisor. Dealer watched closely as his sister listened to her advisor, then slowly lifted her gentle eyes skyward, and smiled. "Are you sure?" she asked cautiously before hanging up the phone.

"Well?" Dealer questioned, squirming in his seat out of curiosity.

"Four million, four hundred thirty one thousand, nine hundred and thirty-six dollars," she muttered slowly, and visions of all the help she could provide for others danced through her mind. Her investment had grown beyond her wildest dreams.

Bess stayed in the town where she was born and raised, using much of her money helping others.

How can $6,750 become a million dollars? The formula worked for all four siblings. The four maximized the formula by investing early, being patient, and using ownership, or rate of return. The options and choices they have now are many. Early use of the formula gave the turtles freedom to pursue their retirement passions.

Benjamin Franklin understood the formula of compound interest. In 1791, he decided to leave $5,000 to the city of Boston. His will specified that the money was to be left untouched without withdrawals for a hundred years.

A hundred years later, in 1891, the account had grown to $322,000. The city fathers used some of the money to build a school and then followed Ben

Franklin's instructions, leaving the rest to compound for another hundred years.

By 1960, the account held $1,400,000 and when the fund ended in 1991, it had grown to almost $5 million.

Ben Franklin's bequest is a great example of how time can multiply a small amount of money into a vast fortune by using compound interest. Ben Franklin (the American father of compound interest, in my opinion) set a fine financial saving example for all Americans more than two hundred years ago.

Rule of 72
How to Calculate Compound Interest

Welcome to the Rule of 72, an easy way to explain compound interest. The Rule of 72 pulls all three components of the formula together. Be mindful, too, that the Rule of 72 is an estimate, not an absolute.

The rule estimates the number of years it takes for an investment's value to double at a specific interest rate, or rate of return.

To perform this calculation, divide 72 by the interest rate; that amount will be the number of years it will take the investment to double. For example, at a rate of 8 percent, an investment's value will double in nine years. Seventy-two divided by eight equals nine.

This measurement is also used to estimate the impact of inflation. At 4 percent inflation, the price of a gallon of milk will double in price in 18 years. Seventy-two divided by four equals eighteen.

The following tables may be helpful in seeing how the Rule of 72 works.

Time and Rate of Return Make a Big Difference

$1,000 will double in this many years	4% 18 years to double	6% 12 years to double	8% 9 years to double	12% 6 years to double
6				$ 2,000
9			$ 2,000	
12		$ 2,000		$ 4,000
18	$ 2,000		$ 4,000	$ 8,000
24		$ 4,000		$16,000
27			$ 8,000	
30				$32,000
36	$ 4,000	$ 8,000	$ 16,000	$64,000

Lump Sum of $50,000

Earning 8% compounded interest on $50,000

Age	35	44	53	62
	$50,000	$100,000	$200,000	$400,000

Earning 12% compounded interest on $50,000

Age	35	41	47	53	59
	$50,000	$100,000	$200,000	$400,000	$800,000

The Rule of 72 is a simple financial planning tool to estimate how much principal you can accumulate at various rates of return. Time and rate make a big difference when measuring the increase in principal. For example, $1,000 grows to $4,000 at four percent, while the same $1,000 grows to $64,000 using 12 percent over the same length of time. What would you rather have—$4,000 or $64,000? Compounding at four percent, the money doubles every eighteen years. But compounding at 12 percent, it doubles every six years.

The best use of compound interest is to use all three components to maximize the results.

Remember, the foundation of compound interest is built on three premises:

a. Save principal regularly.

b. Make certain (keeping in mind that there are risks involved in any kind of investing) your investment earns a fair rate of return.

c. Demonstrate patience, allowing your money to grow. Time is the key. The more time in the compound interest formula, the more money it will produce.

A popular Wall Street investment advisor wrote, "...the relentless wealth-building power of common stock has made millionaires out of countless ordinary people who never in their lives earned a salary that was anything to brag about."

He advised that investors remain in the market; to do otherwise is to miss out on the "greatest wealth-building device ever created. The biggest mistake an investor can make is to avoid it out of some misguided notion of prudence."

He also advised, "...don't wait for the 'right time' to get in on a market 'dip'. It makes no real difference what level the market is when you start investing. Over the long haul, the market has made winners of everyone who has stuck it out long enough." Statistics point clearly to time in the market as more important than market timing.

He told the story of Anne Scheiber, an amateur investor who placed $5,000 in a small number of quality stocks in 1944 and kept them over the long haul. Anne almost never traded, and when she died in 1995, her assets had grown to $22 million—a rate of return, according to him—that sets her alongside Warren Buffett as one of the great investment gurus of all time.

Anne never earned more than $3,150 a year during all her years as an IRS examiner. Still, by the time she passed away, her interest and dividends came to more than $1 million a year.

Summary

- Time is the most important element of compound interest. Savings grow best over long time periods.
- Watch out for investment traps, scams or any of the various forms of gambling.
- Compound interest uses three elements—principal, rate of return, and time, to maximize results.
- Use the Rule of 72 as a financial planning tool to determine the amount of money you can accumulate at various rates of return.

The Cost of Delay:
Waiting to Invest Often Proves Costly

It's a fact that lost time is irretrievable. Gone forever, never to return. In this lesson, the authors talk about time and its value through age perception. They also show that the longer we wait to invest, the more difficult it will be for us to meet our retirement financial goals.

Lost time is never found again.

Benjamin Franklin

Time is your ally, or your enemy. It doesn't care, nor does it differentiate. The law of compound interest also is indifferent. The mathematics of the law demonstrates that the longer you wait to use the formula, the more principal you must contribute to get the same result.

You can pay me now or pay me later, an old television commercial warned us. Putting things off usually costs more.

Monthly Investment	Age
$ 20	25
$ 60	35
$200	45
$850	55

Produces the Same Results at Age 65

Procrastination rarely provides any benefit to the users. Time is fair to all. Each day, time credits each of us with the same 86,400 seconds. And each night, time erases any of it that we fail to use. Time credits us each morning with a fresh batch and each night it wipes the unused balance away.

Lost time is just that; it never returns.

Life is an array of choices that open when we turn age 18. No one gives us a handbook on life. We now make our own decisions. And we are responsible for the results, whether positive or negative.

Procrastination is the thief of time.
Edward Young, poet

73

The Kybalion, a work of Hermetic writings, calls it the law of cause and effect. Every cause has an effect; every effect has a cause; nothing happens by chance. Said another way: as you sow, so shall you reap.

If you plant a seed into the formula of compound interest, you will watch a plant grow. If you don't plant anything, you don't receive anything in return. It's hard to expect a result without a corresponding action.

Our perception of time changes with age. When we are young time drags by. When we are young time moves slowly; time holds us back from the privileges of adulthood. Remember wanting to turn 21?

As we grow older, time flies and the years move faster and faster. Why? Because of our perception of time.

At age ten, a single year equals 10 percent of your total life experience. Ten percent of your life is a long time to wait for your next birthday.

When you reach fifty, one year is only 2 percent of your total life experience. As time moves faster, you try to regain your youth and slow things down. (How does Dick Clark do it?)

It's the feeling of immortality in our youth that causes many people to procrastinate. At that moment, it's easy to believe that life is forever. The perception of time in our youth lures us into a false sense of complacency. No need to think about a retirement that is years and years away. This complacency robs many of the magic of compound interest.

This brings to mind the fable of the grasshopper and the ant:

A live-for-today-and-let-tomorrow-take-care-of-itself grasshopper fluttered leisurely and playfully around the fields all summer long chewing, spitting and inflicting that incessant racket his species make over the entire area.

Meanwhile, his neighbor—an industrious, muscular and quite handsome ant—hot-footed it up and down the dusty road as fast as his several legs could go, sweating up a storm while carrying food (principal, in the formula of compound interest) to be stored at the ant compound.

"What a stupid oaf to work in this heat," the grasshopper said. "It's summer time, and the living is easy."

Well, in short order along comes winter with its icy blasts, leaving the grasshopper cold and hungry, two paychecks away from bankruptcy. Up against it, the grasshopper, shivering because he was shedding his summer skin and suffering for his past indiscretions, paid the ant a visit.

The ant felt compassion for the weakened grasshopper and listened to his tales of woe. The ant grimaced in empathy toward the grasshopper's situation, as the grasshopper declared bankruptcy because he had been laid off at work.

The moral: the ant used the formula of compound interest—he set aside something for the future—the grasshopper didn't.

How many grasshoppers do you know? Or, are you a grasshopper? The ant successfully used the formula and the grasshopper didn't because he failed to save for his future. The ant has more choices, the grasshopper has few.

Success with compound interest is a process. Time and process are the keys to success, using investment wealth as described so poignantly by Dan Millman in his book, The Laws of Spirit.[6]

> If you make today a good day and repeat that process daily, you'll live a lifetime of good days.
>
> Anonymous

"As we washed off our muddy feet and shoes in a stream, the sage offered some advice: 'Remember, Traveler, that lofty dreams in the distant future are a difficult burden to carry. The best goals may be those you can handle in the next week, the next day, the next hour, or the next step; create a process that yields many small successes.'

"Many small successes," I repeated to myself as we continued up a ravine. "But what about people who seem to achieve fame overnight? Where was their process?" I asked the sage.

"Any truly successful venture," she responded, "is like building a house; it begins with a strong foundation and proceeds patiently toward completion. Some houses or careers are built quickly, but without a stable foundation; they look beautiful, but they don't stand for long. If you look closely at 'overnight successes,' you'll find that they usually took about ten years of preparation."

"Ten years…" I said, mostly to myself.

"Think of it," she said. "In ten years, you can accomplish nearly anything. You can become a physician or a scientist. You can develop high-level skills in a sport, game, or martial art. You can become an expert on any subject. You can create wealth or transform your body."

"Ten years still seems like a long time!"

"Looking forward, yes; but looking backward, centuries pass in the snap of a finger, in the blink of an eye."

As Dan describes it ten years may seem like a long time but waiting ten years to start saving is a costly mistake.

The average American worker currently earns $25,000 a year. If you work for forty years you will earn at least a million dollars over your lifetime.

---

[6] From the book **The Laws of Spirit** @ 1995 by Dan Millman. Reprinted by permission of HJ Kramer, P.O. Box 1082, Tiburon, CA 94920. All rights reserved.

MONTHLY INVESTMENT NEEDED TO REPLACE LIFETIME EARNINGS
$25,000 x 40 years = $1,000,000

AGE	MONTHLY INVESTMENT	TOTAL CONTRIBUTION	% OF LIFETIME INCOME	IF YOU WAIT	% NEEDED TO MAKE UP
25	85 X 40 years	$ 40,800	4.08%		
35	287 x 30 years	$ 103,320	10.33%	10 years	253%
45	1,014 x 20 years	$ 243,360	24.33%	20 years	596%
55	4,350 x 10 years	$ 522,000	52.2%	30 years	1,279%

Only the disciplined are free.
James Cash Penney, retailer

If you start a savings plan at age twenty-five you only need to save $85 a month and invest it in equities that compound at 12 percent monthly to accumulate a million dollars to support you through retirement. (This replaces your lifetime income.)

The monthly $85 amounts to only 4.08 percent, or $40,800, of your total lifetime income.

Should you wait to start at age thirty-five, you must save 10.33 percent of your lifetime income, or $103,320, to have the same million dollars at retirement, based on a monthly compounding rate of 12 percent. The monthly savings increase to $287. By waiting ten years, the formula needs 253 percent more principal to produce the same million dollars.

Wait another ten years until age forty-five, and the cost increases 596 percent to $243,360, or 24 percent of your lifetime income to produce the million dollars at retirement. Again, these figures are based on 12 percent compounded monthly. Not many people making $25,000 a year could save $1,014 a month.

Should you wait until age fifty-five, it becomes mathematically impossible to reproduce your lifetime income. If you're earning $25,000 a year, how do you save more than $4,350 a month?

If you are a late starter, this information may be depressing. But it's never too late to start saving for retirement. Life expectancy has increased dramatically over the past fifty years.

The earlier you start, the less principal it takes to replace your lifetime income. The earlier you start, the more available choices you have. Many late starters will have to adjust their retirement expectations and accept a lower lifestyle as they approach their golden years.

"Pay me now or pay me later." The formula doesn't care. It's your choice.

Summary

- Waiting to save costs financially. The sooner you start saving, the more retirement money you'll enjoy.

- The longer you put off saving, the more principal you must produce to reach your retirement goals.

- It's never too late to start a savings program. The earlier you start, the more choices you have available.

LESSON VI

Taxes Reduce Principal:
The Taxman Cometh, Ready or Not

Don't be depressed by taxes. Lesson VI gives you several alternatives to delay paying taxes. What that means is that you can reduce the taxes withdrawn from each paycheck if you have a tax-sheltered savings program. It offers a variety of tax-deferred programs available to choose from and teaches how to save taxes through financial investments.

If you drive a car, I'll tax the street.
If you try to sit, I'll tax your seat.
If you get too cold, I'll tax the heat.
If you take a walk, I'll tax your feet.
Taxman!
Well, I'm the taxman.
Yeah, I'm the taxman.
The Beatles

The first four lessons described compound interest in its purest form; now reality sets in. When you make money in the United States, Uncle Sam wants a part of it.

In an eight-hour workday, you spend the first hour and fifty-five minutes to pay your federal taxes and the next fifty-five minutes to pay state and local taxes.

On average, you spend 35.5 percent of your workday meeting all your federal, state and local tax obligations, according to the Tax Foundation using Department of Commerce data.

Figured another way, you work from January to May each year just to pay your taxes.

Tax freedom day for most families is May 11. Taxes, of course, reduce principal. And the reduction (taxes) leaves less principal to compound.

The impact of taxes reduces the amount the formula can produce. Knowledge of tax laws is an important part of financial success in America. Minimizing the impact of income tax is an important component of wealth accumulation.

When teaching investment classes I ask the participants how many people would like a tax-free loan from the government. Everybody reacts with raised hands. After all, we all want a government handout.

Here's the way it works. For every $3 you contribute, the Federal government gives $1. The government portion is in essence an interest-free loan from Uncle Sam.

Sound like a good deal? If you could get this interest-free loan, how much would you take? As much as you could get? Resounding yes'es come from the voices of the eager students.

The U.S. government gives everybody that opportunity right now. There are a multitude of tax deductible investment options available. They include 401(k)s, 403(b)s, 457s, and Simple IRAs, all of which are payroll-driven through an employer, and the traditional IRAs and SEP accounts that are available to small businesses and individuals.

Whether you are employed or own a business, you have the right to a tax-deductible investment plan.

When you make a contribution to a tax-deductible investment, you defer the taxes until you remove money from your account. If you are in the 25 percent tax bracket, the money that normally would be paid in taxes is available to compound in the formula. The taxes which would have been paid (and would never be seen again) are the interest-free loans.

If you don't use a tax-deferred investment, the taxes are paid up front and that portion of principal is forever lost.

Several of my colleagues were having a discussion recently with a young man in his junior year in college. He was starting the job interview process, and looking for advice on a future career.

The discussion led to career opportunities and someone mentioned that advancement should be one of his main considerations in selecting an employer.

My advice, to everyone's shock, was to review the company's retirement benefits package. Retirement benefits a company offers are one of the keys to financial success for most American workers. If you take a job with a company that doesn't offer a retirement plan, you're fighting an uphill financial battle.

Maximize Tax-Free Loan;
Hide Wages From Taxes

When you start the journey of wealth accumulation, the first principle is to defer or hide current earnings from taxes. Said another way, maximize the interest-free loan from the government. The easiest way is through your paycheck.

There are several payroll-driven retirement plans, 401(k) for companies and non-profit organizations, 403(b) and 457 for government entities, and Simple IRAs for small business.

The money is taken from your paycheck before taxes. Because the contributions are withdrawn pre-tax, you owe less tax.

Assuming you are in the 25 percent tax bracket for each $1,000 invested in a tax-deferred retirement plan, you shave $250 off your tax bill. What's more, the investment grows free of taxes until you take it out.

Payroll-driven plans protect investors from spending temptations that confront us daily. Out of sight, out of mind. The money is taken from the check before you can touch it. This process makes most payroll-driven savers successful. When money is in your checking account it's much more difficult to save. Most Americans have more month than they have paycheck.

Payroll-driven plans are a sure-fire way to pay yourself first. That's sage advice that has been passed down through the centuries.

If you work for a company that has a matching contribution, then your financial success accelerates. Eight of ten employers match some portion of a 401(k) contribution.

If you are contributing a portion of your income and your company matches 25 percent of your contribution, you immediately made 25 percent on your investment. Obviously, the higher the match the faster the account grows. Maximizing your employer's matching contribution is a financial must.

Let's look at an example. If you contribute $100 to a 401(k) and you're in the 25 percent tax bracket, the $100 contribution will reduce your paycheck by only $75. Why?

The contribution reduces your taxable income, thus lowering the taxes you owe. Your income did not really decline; the money normally sent to the government is transferred into your account to earn interest.

With the full $100 going into your 401(k) the company matches your contribution with $25. Therefore, your paycheck drops by $75 and $125 is put in your account—your $100 plus the $25 match. If your company matches 50 percent, then $75 is out of your check and $150 goes into your 401(k) account. The match is exciting. Where else can you take $75 out of your check and have $125 or $150 deposited in an investment?

Can you see why my advice to the student was to check out the potential employer's retirement benefits? Who you choose to work for is an important career decision.

If you don't have a payroll-driven option, you are entitled to contribute to a traditional IRA account. The tax advantages of the IRA are the same as the payroll-driven plan, except you are limited to only a $2,000 contribution each year.

The traditional IRA takes more self-discipline. You must save after-tax dollars from your checkbook. The $2,000 is a tax deduction that you receive when you file your income tax.

Self-employed and small business owners can open Simplified Employer Plan (SEP) IRAs, which works like a traditional IRA. The SEP is geared toward net income (income minus expenses) and allows higher contributions in some circumstances.

The government would never offer an interest-free loan without strings attached. If funds are withdrawn prior to age 59 1/2, the amount taken is subject to a 10 percent penalty plus taxes. Some rules have recently been liberalized to allow withdrawals for first time home purchases and for educational expenses. It's important to consult with a tax advisor before making any withdrawal before age 59 1/2.

Don't get confused with all the options. Your first goal is to explore and maximize your entitled tax deduction, thus broadening your interest-free loan.

Hide Your Investment Earnings From Taxes

After you have executed your tax-free loan, the second strategy is to avoid being taxed twice.

If you have saved some after-tax principal now make sure that the investment earnings or investment income are not taxed again. The taxes can be delayed until the investor decides to spend some of the principal.

There are three tax control options:

1. Tax deferral, through annuities.
2. Capital gains, through common stock.
3. Tax-free growth, through municipal bonds and Roth IRAs.

None of these options furnishes a tax deduction but each does provide the ability for the investor to control the taxes of the investment.

Make the Right Tax Deferral Choice

One choice of tax deferral is through an insurance product called an annuity. There are two common types of annuities—fixed and variable.

Fixed annuities offer an investment return similar to certificates of deposit and government bonds. With a fixed return, the principal doesn't fluctuate. The historical returns are lower because an investor is lending money to the insurance company.

Variable annuities offer various investment categories. If you choose equity, the principal will fluctuate and will most likely produce higher rates of return over time.

Annuities provide investors with the option to pay taxes when they choose to withdraw the funds. When funds are withdrawn, taxes are paid only on the amount distributed. The remainder of the balance is sheltered from taxes each year. Let's look at an example.

Jim and Jane each invest $50,000 for thirty years earning 8 percent annually. Jim puts his initial investment in a tax-deferred account; Jane places hers in a non tax-deferred investment. She pays her taxes each year.

Thirty years later Jim's initial $50,000 investment grew to about $503,133. Though not as fortunate, Jane's $50,000 investment had grown to $218,082. Each year, Jane's tax bill grew higher and higher.

Taxable Investment

Year	8% return	Tax	Total value of contract (principal + earnings taxes)
0			$ 50,000
1	$ 4,000	$ 1,484	$ 52,516
2	$ 4,201	$ 1,559	$ 55,159
3	$ 4,413	$ 1,637	$ 57,934
4	$ 4,635	$ 1,719	$ 60,849
5	$ 4,868	$ 1,806	$ 63,911
30	$16,611	$ 6,163	$218,082

Tax-Deferred Annuity

Year	8% return	Tax	Total value of contract (principal + earnings)
0			$ 50,000
1	$ 4,000	$ 0	$ 54,000
2	$ 4,320	$ 0	$ 58,320
3	$ 4,666	$ 0	$ 62,986
4	$ 5,039	$ 0	$ 68,024
5	$ 5,442	$ 0	$ 73,466
30	$37,269	$ 0	$503,133

Over thirty years Jim has more than twice the amount of Jane. The power of tax-deferral is working in his favor.

But Jim still owes taxes on his investment. If Jim were to withdraw all of his funds at once, he would pay a lot of tax, but he would still be substantially ahead of Jane.

A recent study from PricewaterhouseCoopers to the National Association for Variable Annuities concluded that for holding periods as short as ten years, after-tax payouts funded by variable annuities were larger than mutual funds or by other taxable investments.

The study illustrates an investor in the 20 percent tax rate during accumulation, and in the 15 percent bracket at distribution. Most working taxpayers will retire in a lower tax bracket. The longer the tax-deferred holding period, the greater the financial results.

The study showed that using tax-deferral for a ten-year holding period produced a 20 percent better outcome than its taxable counterpart. The fifteen-year holding period was 63 percent better and the twenty-year holding period was 164 percent better than paying taxes as you go.

It's been my experience that investors don't withdraw large sums of money from tax-deferred accounts because they want to avoid paying taxes. Most investors take only what they need. The study further states that if you withdraw money slowly through systematic withdrawal, the results are even more dramatic. Systematic withdrawal is taking a monthly or quarterly withdrawal on a regular basis.

The difference using the ten-year systematic withdrawal produced a 167 percent benefit over the tax-as-you-go account. Fifteen years is 510 percent greater and twenty years is 1,165 percent more return than paying taxes each year.

Annuities can provide wealth accumulation through tax-deferral but they do have some drawbacks. If the earnings are withdrawn before age 59 1/2, the government imposes a 10 percent penalty similar to the tax-deductible strategies, and income taxes are due in the year of the withdrawal.

Annuities are somewhat controversial in the investment community. Many critics claim that they have too many fees. The insurance industry counterclaims that the fees are justified because they provide insurance against investment loss of principal.

The important thing to remember is the power of tax-deferral. The government doesn't give investors many ways to hide investment earnings from taxes.

Use Investments to Delay Paying Taxes

Investing in common stock offers investors another choice to avoid paying taxes.

When you purchase shares in ABC Company, you don't pay taxes until you sell. If you decide not to sell, you can avoid income tax on the increase altogether.

If you were one of the original Microsoft investors, your initial investment might be worth millions of dollars. The increase of value will not be taxed until you decide to sell. If you decide not to sell, you don't pay the tax. The investor is in control of the tax consequences.

For investments held longer than a year, taxpayers receive a lower tax rate called a capital gain. Capital gain taxes are significantly lower than ordinary income taxes.

The maximum tax rate on a capital gain is 20 percent compared to ordinary income tax rates as high as 39.6 percent. In lower income tax brackets, the capital gain rate declines to 10 percent or below.

If you hold a common stock for longer than five years, starting in the year 2001 the capital gain rate drops to 18 percent in the highest bracket and to 8 percent in the lowest.

Common stock offers one of the best tax avoidance strategies to investors, with preferential tax rates when the stock is held over one year. Avoiding investment tax is one of the ways Bill Gates and Warren Buffet have become among the richest people in the world.

Tax-Free Options: Muni Bonds and the Roth IRAs

For more than a hundred years wealthy investors have been investing in tax-free municipal bonds, a fixed income investment that pays interest every six months.

Because bonds are issued and sold by state and local governments, the interest income is not taxed to the owners. The tax advantage allows schools and other government entities to finance public infrastructure projects at a lower interest rate.

Municipal bonds offer a high degree of safety and are popular with conservative investors in high tax brackets. In some states a tax-free bond is equivalent to earning 9 percent on a taxable investment when the state and federal income tax are combined.

If you are in a lower income bracket, then municipal bonds lose their appeal because taxable bonds or common stock will provide greater after-tax returns.

Roth IRA: Tax Free
Compounding Using Equities

It must have been late at night when Senator William Roth pushed his savings program bill through the Senate in Washington, D. C. Here's what the program offers:

- For the first time, U.S. investors can use equity returns to compound principal totally free of taxes.

- Roth IRAs are treated the same as ordinary IRAs; you must have earned income to make contributions. The contributions of Roth IRAs are non-deductible and the maximum contribution is $2,000 yearly.

- Although the Roth does not provide front-end tax savings, the back-end rewards are exciting. If you hold the Roth for at least five years, the withdrawals from the account are free of income tax when the owner has reached the age of 59 1/2.

- Different than the traditional IRA, Roth owners are not forced to take distributions at age 70 1/2. The Roth is subject to income ceilings. Under current law for single taxpayers, the adjusted gross income phase-outs start at $95,000, and for joint tax filers it starts at $150,000. The legislation restricts high income earners from this tax-free accumulation vehicle.

- The Roth also offers a conversion feature whereby account holders can convert traditional IRAs, pay the taxes now (reduce principal) and grow the account tax-free going forward. You don't need earned income to convert an existing IRA, but if your earnings are over $100,000, you can't convert an existing IRA. Whether to convert is a complicated matter; be sure to analyze the numbers before making this irrevocable decision.

The Roth benefits young investors. Young savers through the miracle of compound interest will be more likely to be in higher tax brackets at retirement. The Roth IRA would work very well for the four-investment turtles in Lesson IV. Children must have earned income to be eligible to make Roth contributions.

Parents or grandparents could convert part of their traditional IRAs and name their children or grandchildren as beneficiaries. A $2,000 Roth IRA invested in equities would grow to over a million dollars for a newborn grandchild if the child holds the principal to age 65.

The Roth IRA offers considerable opportunities for families who wish to create generational wealth.

Beat the Government

If you are a late starter in the wealth accumulation process and you don't want to work forever, there's still hope. As mentioned in the variable annuity study, most retirees

watch their tax bills decline the day they retire. If you are turning age 50, your best option is to maximize your tax free loan using IRA's or payroll deduction, making contributions in a high tax bracket, and taking distributions in a low tax bracket.

It reminds me of a client named Lester Pitman. Lester started his 401(k) at age fifty-five. He had a small balance from an old profit-sharing plan.

Lester was in the 28 percent tax bracket and for ten years put as much as the government would allow into his 401(k) account until he reached age sixty-five, when he retired.

Lester applied for Social Security and was eligible for $12,000 a year. He also started taking $1,000 a month from his retirement account. Currently, Lester receives $24,000 a year and pays no income tax. As long as he withdraws his money slowly, he can avoid income tax during his lifetime. He is able to keep the taxes he would have paid to Uncle Sam and enjoy the tax savings in his retirement years. Lester truly is using the tax system to his advantage.

Let's take it a step farther and assume that Lester is married. Here's what his total yearly retirement package would look like after standard federal tax deductions for a married couple.

Standard deduction for a married couple . . . .**$ 8,900**

Personal exemption for Lester . . . .**$ 2,750**

Personal exemption for Lester's wife . . . .**$ 2,750**

Lester can withdraw up to $14,400 from his retirement account without paying tax. As long as his total income stays below $32,000 he will not pay taxes on his Social Security.

This chapter is not designed to be a complete handbook on IRAs and other tax strategies. It's our goal to present the general concepts of tax deferral.

Congress has changed the laws so many times that a whole book could be dedicated to the rules and to their changes and exceptions. It's best to review your personal situation with a professional to get the best tax information and direction.

I have witnessed many people who didn't have a clue about the tax implications of their investments. That lack of knowledge can be costly. Many

Americans needlessly give their hard-earned money back to the government in the form of taxes, never to be seen again.

Summary

- Taxes cut back the amount of principal compound interest can produce.
- Make use of the available tax deductible investment options now available such as 401(k)s, 403(b)s, 457s, Simple IRAs and others.
- All employee contributions to a tax-deductible investment are tax-deferred until you move the money from your account.
- Without a tax-deferred investment plan, taxes are paid up front and principal is lost.
- Hide your investment earnings from taxes through annuities, common stock, or through municipal bonds and Roth IRAs.

LESSON VII

How to Make Major
Principal Decisions

Lesson VII centers on how to examine major buying decisions such as purchase of a home, automobile and other big-ticket items. The authors offer money-saving programs that will help take the stress from the large mortgage payments of such purchases.

*When you understand that every choice has an end result, you place
yourself in a position to become successful in every area of your life.*

Anonymous

When you analyze your working career and look at your total earnings
power, there are a couple of financial decisions that could have a big impact
on your financial success.

As in Lesson V, when you take your annual income and multiple it by forty
years, you get some idea of how much money, in today's dollars, you'll gen-
erate in your working lifetime.

Inflation will increase your earnings over time, but it will also increase
your expenses. If you make $25,000 a year and work forty years, that pro-
duces a $1 million in pretax earnings. When you look at your total lifetime
earnings and review your options, it takes on a different meaning. How will
you spend your million dollars?

Remember when you earn a million dollars, the government wants its
share in the form of taxes. They'll take between $100,000 and $150,000 right
off the top. (That's why tax deferral is a great avenue to financial success).

That means after taxes you'll have about $900,000 to spend in the game
of life. It's important to be an informed consumer. When you work, you are
trading your time and energy for the money you earn. When the money is
spent, you have exchanged your energy for goods and services. Is it a fair
exchange?

Many consumers don't examine the economic consequences of their purchase decisions. If you only have $900,000 to spend over the course of your
working life, it's important to get the best bang for your bucks. Of course
there are necessities in life such as food and shelter.

Let's look first at shelter.

Buying A Home

I believe that owning a home is one of the best investments you will ever make.

A home is a form of ownership (equity). Ownership over time increases in value; ownership in a home is even encouraged by the government. One good thing about home ownership is that the interest expenses from home mortgages are tax-deductible once the interest exceeds the standard deduction.

Recent legislation makes the gain on the sale of your primary residence tax-free if you follow the guidelines. (Wow, tax-free appreciation, another way to grow tax-free principal.)

Home ownership is a sign of stability. Nearly everyone you do business with will ask if you rent or own a home.

Home ownership is a forced savings plan. Many people who have trouble saving will make their monthly house payments. After thirty years of making house payments, they have accumulated a substantial net worth because (barring refinancing or home equity loans) the property has increased in value and the mortgage has been paid.

Owning a home is a driving economic force in America. Seldom does the value of real estate decrease, and home loans can be secured, usually on fifteen-year or thirty-year fixed mortgages, at reasonable interest rates from 7 to 9 percent.

When you buy a home, it's prudent to consider a fifteen-year mortgage. What are its advantages? Probably the biggest is that you save a considerable amount of interest expense by cutting in half the number of payments you'll make. That alone is a large selling point for some folks.

Here's a quick way to compare the cost of a thirty-year fixed versus a fifteen-year fixed mortgage:

Take the monthly payments for each loan and calculate the total price of the home. Multiply the fifteen-year loan payment by 180 to get the total cost of the home. Do the same for the thirty-year loan but multiply by 360 payments. Subtract the two totals and the difference is the extra interest paid for the same home.

An example:

Loan Amount	Monthly Payments		Total Payments	
(@ 9% interest)	30 year fixed	15 year fixed	30 year fixed	15 year fixed
$150,000	$1,206.93	$1,521.39	$434,494.80	$273,850.20
			The difference $160,644.60	
(@ 8% interest)				
$150,000	$1,100.65	$1,433.48	$396,234.00	$258,026.40
			The difference $138,207.60	
(@ 7% interest)				
$150,000	$ 997.95	$1,348.24	$359,262.00	$242,683.20
			The difference $116,578.80	

In the example using 8 percent interest, the difference is $138,207 for selecting a fifteen-year mortgage versus one for thirty years. The increased monthly payment is more than $300 a month.

By choosing the higher payments you save $138,207 of your lifetime earnings. The thirty-year mortgage would cost $396,234 of your lifetime earnings. What would you do with the $138,207?

The extra money would dramatically increase the financial options of most Americans. If you were to plug that $138,207 into the compound interest formula it wouldn't be hard to retire financially independent.

Some financial planners would advocate always having a mortgage during your working career. Others advocate that renting produces higher financial returns. Home ownership is a personal choice, but financing over fifteen years can save you a lot of dough.

THE IRON CHARIOT

Most of America must invest in transportation in order to earn a living. It's estimated that on average, Americans will drive over 900,000 miles in his or her lifetime.

The American Automobile Association estimates that the average cost to own (wear and tear) and to operate (fuel) a car is 45¢ a mile. That means that the average American will spend approximately $405,000 on transportation. The IRS, incidentally, allows 32.5¢ a mile.

If you drive 15,000 miles a year multiplied by .45¢ a mile, multiplied by forty years–that equates to $270,000 of your lifetime income (15,000 x .45¢ x 40 years = $270,000).

Cars are a way of life for Americans. Many financial planners advocate buying a used car versus a new one. Either that, or drive your existing car longer. If you choose one of those strategies, it's estimated that you can save over $2,000 a year: $2,000 times forty years times 10 percent equals $1,041,394. If you put the money into an employer 401(k) plan with a 25 percent matching contribution, it grows to $1,301,742.

According to Thomas Stanley and William Kanko, authors of The Millionaire Next Door, 37 percent of all millionaires bought a used vehicle as their most recent car. And 25 percent of those millionaires hadn't purchased a new car in four years or more.

Other Principal-Saving Ideas

There are multitudes of ways to save money to plug into the compound interest formula. Many of them sound like a parent or a doctor telling people things they don't want to hear, such as "don't smoke," or "don't drink," or "don't eat junk food." Before you roll your eyes to the back of your head, a modest change in certain habits can be the fuel that ignites financial success.

Healthy Savings - Compounded Monthly

Description	Interest	Time Period	Total	401(k) 25% Match
Smoking a pack a day Save $3/day x 365 days	10%	40 years	$577,072.26	$721,324.54
Drinking two six-packs a week Save $40/month x 12 months	10%	40 years	$252,963.18	$316,203.98
Saving $1.50/day on junk food Save $1.50/day x 365 days	10%	40 years	$288,567.75	$360,725.50

Make saving principal a game. Involve everyone. Have a common goal; involve the family.

When you add the total cost of home ownership ($434,494) and the total cost of transportation ($270,000), you can see why most working families need two incomes to get by in today's society.

Ben Franklin was America's first consumer advocate. Through his writings—he always talked about a fictitious character that went by the name of

Poor Richard—Ben Franklin encouraged Americans to be financially thrifty.

One of Poor Richard's famous quotes was that even "a small leak can sink a great ship."

Let's look at some other small leaks that most people don't think about.

Practical Savings - Compounded Monthly

Description	Interest	Time Period	Total	401(k) 25% Match
Don't play the lottery Save $250 a year	10%	40 years	$131,749.55	$164,691.68
Clip grocery coupons $5/week Save $5/week x 52 weeks	10%	40 years	$137,023.83	$171,275.05
Term life insurance vs. whole life Save $600 x year	10%	40 years	$316,203.98	$395,254.97

Oh, by the way, I didn't mention premium coffee because I love the stuff and that's the author's prerogative.

How consumers spend their lifetime income is a personal choice. Many consumers spend all of their earnings and leave nothing for the formula of compound interest. When investors set aside enough capital to replace their lifetime income, they can retire or pursue other passions in life.

This chapter offers a few strategies to save money, and there are many more. Whether it's a 15-year mortgage or clipping grocery coupons, by saving money and using compound interest, you'll move down the road to financial freedom.

Summary

- Examine the financial consequences of any major principal decision.
- Home ownership is equity, a sign of stability and a forced savings plan.
- When buying a home, consider a 15-year mortgage instead of the more popular 30-year mortgage and realize a huge saving.
- Watch for the little saving items that make a difference.

LESSON VIII

Never Pay an Interest Rate Higher Than You Can Earn

The key to Lesson VIII is to avoid debt if possible. If you're in debt, pay it off as quickly as feasible. As you pay off each debt, try and save the payments you were making on each debt. The authors discuss prepayments on debt, especially credit cards—which usually charge an interest rate of 14 to 24 percent.

I'd rather go to bed supperless, than rise in debt.

Benjamin Franklin

Compound interest doesn't discriminate; it's available to lenders and investors.

The demand for credit has created a multibillion dollar banking and finance industry. Ownership in the lending industry has provided some of the best investment returns on Wall Street. Why? Because the pay as you go consumer keeps financing more and more items.

When a consumer borrows money the lending company assesses the risk to the financial institution. The higher the risk the higher the interest rate that is charged. The higher the net worth, (assets minus debts equals net worth), the better the credit risk, the lower the interest rate charged.

When I graduated from college in 1980 and needed a car, I was charged 24 percent interest. I had zero net worth. My banker said he was doing me a favor. I never worked so hard in my life to pay off a loan.

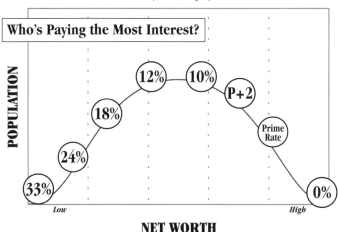

The higher the credit risks, the higher the interest rate charged. The higher the charged finance rate, the higher the finance costs. The higher the finance cost, the higher the financed item cost—using more of your lifetime income.

Bankers Rule of 72

24%	—	debt doubles in 3 years
18%	—	debt doubles in 4 years
12%	—	debt doubles in 6 years
10%	—	debt doubles in 7 years
9%	—	debt doubles in 8 years

As you can see, the lending industry offers attractive returns to investors. Add loan origination costs, late payment charges and the annual fee renewals, and the return to the lender increases. The interest expense paid reduces the amount of principal the borrower has to accumulate wealth. Besides, it increases the total cost of the item purchased.

Before you buy something, multiply all the payments for the term of the loan to determine the true cost, as we did purchasing a home; $396,234 versus $150,000 borrowed is a big difference. The same concept should be used on smaller purchases.

It reminds me of Miss Mini.

A young woman named Minimum Payment (friends call her Miss Mini) got a phone call one day. It was one of her ten credit card companies who coldly informed her that she had reached a $3,500 card limit, and she was to cease and desist using the little plastic money gobbler or return it posthaste. The card carried an interest rate of 17 percent.

Soon after, Miss Mini's next monthly statement landed in the mailbox, informing her that her minimum payment was $70. That suited Miss Mini just fine, because it fell in line with another of her misguided customs—never pay a penny more each month than what the statement required.

That evening, depressed because of her credit card debt and her financial misfortune in general, Miss Mini got out her digital calculator and with a fury started punching in numbers. A few minutes later, she realized that if she immediately stopped all use of the card, and if she mailed each required minimum payment on time with no missed or partial payments or late penalties, she'd end up owing $11,162 instead of the $3,500 she initially rang up.

She was astounded and more than slightly irked. Why, that's over three times the amount of money she had charged to her card. Sweating profusely from stress—not because of her calculator exercise—Miss Mini felt short of breath and got herself a drink of water. Then she cried.

Easy credit is the demise of many consumers. Many lay prey to the tempting offers of buy now and pay later. Aesop's fable of the grasshopper and the ant was never more true than when applied to the consumer credit industry.

Grasshoppers live for today, not tomorrow.

Grasshoppers can't delay the immediate gratification of a new purchase. Their common cry is "live for the day."

Grasshoppers suffer from the Minimum Payment Syndrome and want to know what they can afford, not what it costs.

Grasshoppers are suckers for low payment plans and deferred interest charges.

Grasshoppers jump from credit card to credit card, playing financial musical chairs until the music stops and they're stuck paying high interest rates. When summer ends, the grasshoppers' depreciated toys are still costing them money.

The classified ads and pawnshops are full of grasshoppers' past indulgences.

Investment ants can get good deals on boats in the winter and snow toys in the summer.

> Creditors have better memories than debtors.
> Benjamin Franklin

Grasshoppers pay the highest interest rates because they don't have any assets (net worth); they're loaded down with debt. If they miss a payment they lower their credit rating and pay even higher rates.

Grasshoppers have higher divorce rates; 70 percent of divorced couples cite money as the main culprit.

Many grasshoppers are two paychecks removed from bankruptcy; they have no choice but to go to work every day in order to maintain their lifestyle.

If you know any grasshoppers out there in today's society, there is one simple rule ants use that grasshoppers don't: "Never pay a higher interest rate than you can earn."

Credit Cards, A Plastic Prison

Consumer credit has experienced tremendous growth. The average American has eight to ten credit cards. Credit card companies send out 3.5 billion solicitations a year. That's not hard to believe; I received over thirty invitations in less than a month's time—not counting three phone call pitches at dinner.

America's "grasshoppers" currently hold over $455 billion in credit card debt. Charge card volume has increased from a staggering $338 billion in 1990 to a projected $975 billion in 1999. Studies show that consumers spend 23 percent more using a credit card than if they had paid cash.

The deferral of making a credit card payment for thirty days gives a false sense of financial liability. The same 30-day period coupled with the low monthly payments lures many consumers into credit card bondage. Ever wonder why it takes so long to pay off the balance? Some credit cards have long payment schedules, many up to fifteen years if only the minimum payment is sent in on time.

But there's a new kid on the block. Another payment calculation credit card companies have adopted is the principle of 36. The concept is perpetual debt. Here's how it works. The credit card companies take 1/36 of the balance, plus the interest, to calculate your payments. The thirty-six months payment plan never ends unless you add extra principal to the payment.

Talk about financial bondage. Looking from the credit card companies' perspective, you wouldn't want the debt balance to ever be paid off either. At 18 to 24 percent interest, credit card companies double their money every three to four years.

The interest expense paid for consumer purchases could be the principal used to become financially independent. If you are in debt and want to turn the law of compound interest in your favor, the best plan is to list your debts according to interest rates from highest to lowest.

First, pay off the debt with the highest interest rate. Then, once that debt is out of the way, take both payments to pay off the next highest debt. Use this procedure until you have paid off any debt that is higher than you can earn in a long-term investment strategy.

The only exception to debt reduction is if you work for an employer that offers a matching contribution through a payroll savings plan. Taking advantage of the maximum matching contribution, then plow the rest against a high interest debt to produce the best financial outcome.

Prepayments: When to Use Them

Debt is like cholesterol; there is good debt and bad debt. There are two types of bad debt: debt on items that depreciate in value, and debt that charges a higher interest rate than you can earn in a long-term investment portfolio.

Finance Company	%	Bad Debt	Interest Tax Deductible
High Finance Company	24%	Yes	No
Low Grade Credit Card	18%	Yes	No
Average Credit Card	16%	Yes	No
Premium Credit Card	12%	Yes	No
Home Equity Loan	8-10%	No	Yes
Home Mortgage	7%	No	Yes

Debt on your home (an equity item), a form of ownership, is good because equity investments over time increase in value, and the interest expense is tax deductible once the interest expense exceeds the standard deduction.

Investors are always looking for the perfect investment. Something that pays a high rate of return and is guaranteed. Prepaying high interest rate debt (bad debt) is the best guaranteed return. Pay it off as fast as you can.

If Miss Mini, for example, were to add $3 a month to her payment she would save over $1,800 dollars and start her move down the road to financial freedom.

Should I Pay Off My Home Early?

When an investor becomes debt-free he or she has the maximum financial freedom. Paying off your home early boils down to personal choice versus a financial choice.

If money is the only criterion, renting while investing the down payment and the difference in lower monthly rent payments will produce the highest financial return. Having your home paid for is a great feeling and improves your net worth. But it's important to note that equity in your home is not an earning asset. It's "dead" equity, a non-income producing asset.

The only way a home will produce income is if you sell your home and move into a smaller place, investing the proceeds to produce income or using a reverse mortgage. A cursory look at the reverse mortgage clearly puts the advantage to the lender and not to the homeowner.

If you choose to prepay your mortgage, it is amazing how a little additional principal produces big savings. The extra payment reduces the interest expense, thus shortening the length of the loan. Many baby boomers are aggressively pre-paying the mortgages on their homes, preparing for retirement. Having your home paid off reduces monthly living expenses, making it easier to retire.

Before prepaying a mortgage, it's important to remember that an employer's retirement plan with a matching contribution is a better financial choice than prepaying good debt.

The next choice is nondeductible high interest rate debt (bad debt).

If you choose to pay off your home, "a little dab'll do ya." Small additions to your mortgage payment will create big savings.

Small Pre-Payments Make a Big Difference
Based on $100,000 Mortgage
at 8% for 30 years

Pre-Pay	Save
$ .10 per day	$ 3,317
$ .25 per day	$ 7,986
$ .50 per day	$15,054
$1.00 per day	$27,072

Parents and grandparents are occasionally in a financial position to reward their offspring. Many are hesitant to give an outright gift of cash or securities to novice investors fearing they might act like young grasshoppers.

My suggestion is to leverage the gift by applying the gift to the child's mortgage or help with the down payment for a home. Apply the gift to a mortgage and the gifts will multiply several times by reducing the length of the loan and reducing the amount of interest paid over the life of the loan. Equity in a home is also hard to spend. Although it may not be the most financially astute decision, it is a great way to help children that have not developed much financial discipline.

How you spend your lifetime income is a personal choice. Becoming an informed consumer puts you in a position to achieve multiple financial goals. Whether it's a home, a car or small items such as playing the lottery or smoking cigarettes, the principal you spend and how you allocate your lifetime earnings will determine when and if you will ever experience financial freedom.

If you are a grasshopper and can't discipline your spending habits, you get trapped in the financial web of bad debt and become mired in the same formula that, used correctly, could make you wealthy.

To use a Star Wars analogy, you are living on the dark side of the formula: principal X rate of return X time. The country should thank you for helping fuel the economy.

Come to the light and experience the economic freedom and choice that investment ants experience.

May the force be with you. Or, may the formula be with you.

Summary

- Never pay a higher interest rate than an investment will earn.
- Don't run up excessive credit card debt; it's deadly for those serious about investment savings.
- Be systematic about paying off credit card debt; pay off first the debt with the highest interest rate. That accomplished, use both payments (the one you made, and the savings from the payoff) and tackle the next highest debt.
- Prepaying a mortgage often produces big savings through reduced interest expense, which shortens the loan.
- Small home mortgage prepayments make a big savings.

LESSON IX

Exponential Compounding: Proper Use of Formula Equals Financial Success

Have you ever seen or done something that illustrated a case in point, or an object lesson? Something that makes you want to do better, or to straighten up and fly right? Makes you want to try harder or improve on something you think you already do well? This lesson tells of exponential compounders for those who want to improve themselves. The writers offer lists of tangible, activity-based self-improvement, and warn of barriers that might get in the way.

If you don't know what you want in life, you probably won't achieve much.

Sir John Templeton

Why is common sense uncommon?

Goals and plans have been the foundation for financial success or any type of achievement for centuries. If you ask most people where they are going in life, they can't tell you.

A 1997 study by Employee Benefits Research Institute (EBRI) revealed that only 36 percent of current workers have tried to determine how much they need to save for a comfortable retirement. Of those who tried, 24 percent could not give a figure when asked. That means that three-quarters of all current workers do not know how much money they will need at retirement.

The study asked "why" of those workers that neglected to determine their retirement needs. Twenty-nine percent responded that they were afraid to find out, 20 percent said the process was too complicated, and 39 percent noted lack of time.

It's easy to understand, then, why a 1997 study by Public Agenda found that nearly half of all Americans have less than $10,000 saved for retirement.

Many consumers spend more time planning their yearly vacations than they do on their financial futures. Today, because of the trends of early retirement and longer life expectancy, the average American can expect to spend more than 20 percent of his or her life in retirement.

It's not hard to believe that people with investment plans have more than those with-

> *At this exact moment, you are where you are because of the choices you have made in your life.*
> Anonymous

111

out. People with employer-driven retirement plans are light years ahead of most Americans.

As a financial advisor, the common question asked by all potential retirees is, "how much is enough?" Well, the longer you wait for that answer, the more principal it takes to produce the outcome.

But there's a hidden cost, too. The longer the delay, the more guilt and anxiety you feel. It's a silent pressure that most people won't admit to, but it's there all the same. I know the feeling firsthand.

A few years back, I found myself constantly helping parents establish college savings plans for their children. Yet I hadn't started similar plans for my own children, ages three and five at the time.

> *Even if you're on the right track, you'll get run over if you just sit there.*
> Will Rogers, humorist

Every time I helped someone else, the gnawing knowledge of my procrastination became stronger and stronger. The guilt of inaction combined with watching my children get older was too much to bear and the stress was unbelievable. Finally, I took a positive action, established a monthly savings plan, and the stress disappeared. I now have in place a savings vehicle for my children's educational future. I felt like a million bucks at the time I put their educational plans in place, and still do every time I think about it.

Why don't most people write down goals? Goals are easy to say, but hard to achieve. Do you have something you want to accomplish? Put this book down, take out a clean sheet of paper and write down a goal. Set a timeline and initiate a list of "action steps" to accomplish it. Sound easy?

It's not. Most people freeze. It's a personal commitment. It's difficult to sign a personal contract and hold yourself accountable. Once you've committed to an outcome, you feel the responsibility to work toward accomplishing your goals, For the first time, you might fail and fall flat on your face. If you never set a goal, you can't fail. People without goals don't have to be responsible to anything or anybody—even themselves.

> *You may be disappointed if you fail, but you are doomed if you don't try.*
> Beverly Sills, opera singer and administrator

In 1950, several Ivy League colleges took on a study of that year's graduating classes. One of the questions asked of the graduates was whether they had set firm life goals. Eighty-seven percent responded no; 10 percent said they had set mental goals but had not committed them to writing. Only 3 percent had put their life goals in writing.

The schools monitored the graduates for twenty-five years, and, in 1975, found that the 87 percent who held no goals had average levels of achievement. The 10 percent who kept their goals in their minds instead of on paper outperformed the 87 percent group. The 3 percent who had written goals, however, had outdistanced them all. They had accumulated more assets than the entire 97 percent.

Amazing, isn't it, that the 3 percent with clear direction and a signed personal contract had outperformed the rest of the class combined? How can that happen?

Exponential Compounding: Believe In It

When you mix self-improvement with compound interest, the opportunities in life multiply exponentially. It makes sense that if you improve yourself, you can improve your income. Of course, as you increase your income the amount of money that can be saved increases, too.

> *You always pass failure on the way to success.*
> Mickey Rooney, actor

If you take those savings and put them in the formula of compound interest, your investment nest egg will multiply faster. The cost of self-improvement is cheap. You can find thousands of books on the subject at your public library (you can't beat the price), and we all can use a little self-improvement. Self-improvement works at any age; it doesn't discriminate.

When I started reading an hour a day, I decided to study the human brain and its application on self-improvement. I'd always kept mental goals and had a general direction in life, but wanted to move to the next level of achievement.

I started to experiment with the improvement concepts that I learned through reading. I felt like Thomas Edison, conducting experiment after experiment.

When I committed my mental goals to paper, I noticed that my goals kept moving closer and closer to the desired outcome.

As the experiments continued, I started having small successes. With my small successes, my belief in the written goals grew stronger and stronger. As my beliefs grew stronger, the execution of the written goals became easier.

> *You are never given a dream without also being given the power to make it true. You may have to work for it, however.*
> Richard Bach, author of "Jonathan Livingston Seagul"

Let me share an example. In 1989, when my family moved to Coeur d' Alene, I knew my income level would drop. I was starting a new partnership and would need to work hard to rebuild my business. Before the move, I read Napoleon Hill's book, "Think and Grow Rich." The book said to write down your goal every morning and every night.

Each night before I went to bed I wrote my income goal, a figure that was two and a half times more than I had ever made before. I did this for thirty days, until one night my wife asked what I was doing. She looked over my shoulder and read my goal. Then she predicted that I'd never accomplish that goal.

I hate telling this story because you might get the wrong impression about my biggest supporter (my wife) of more than 18 years.

But as you start on the path of self-improvement, sometimes the people closest to you may challenge the process until you produce actual results.

I felt embarrassed at the time and stopped writing my goals. I kept the little sheet of paper, however, and continued to work hard. Many amazing things happened over the next two years, and my business became quite successful.

In 1991, when I received my final December paycheck, the total income for the year had exceeded the goal I had written down two years earlier by $185. I was in shock and looked in the mirror in amazement. How had that happened, or was it just a coincidence?

The next day I committed to several new written goals. I have used them ever since, and written goals are still working the same magic that they did in 1989. I had found the fountain of success that had alluded me earlier in my career.

Self-Improvement Works

For those on a self-improvement path, Hill's book is a must-read. When I met Mark Victor Hansen in 1989 he said he'd read the book more than two hundred times. If you read the book, you'll understand why Hansen and Jack Canfield have been successful with their own books.

I've only read Hill's book fourteen times. My copy is almost worn out with parts of it highlighted and other parts marked with paperclips.

Hill gives readers a roadmap to personal success. The book's general principles are for people to obtain knowledge, apply what you know, believe in the outcome and don't give up.

The concepts Hill describes in his book have been used successfully by ordinary people who consistently applied his principles and became successful.

For exponential compounders starting the path of self-improvement, Hill's book may be too much of a leap at first. It moves quickly from tangible to intangible concepts. Beginners may find intangible concepts too much of a stretch at first, similar to a seventh grader moving into a master's degree at Harvard University.

As I review my life, I found logical steps of self-improvement that slowly moved from the tangible to the intangible. The process is like walking up a flight of stairs. Each step moves you closer to the top and gives you time to integrate

> The rung of a ladder was never meant to rest upon, but only to hold a man's foot long enough to enable him to put the other somewhat higher.
> Thomas H. Huxley, biologist

and digest what you learned at the last level. Take a walk up the stairs of self-improvement. As you walk the stairs, watch your income increase and fulfill exponential compounding.

Staircase of Self-Improvement:
Tangible, activity-based self-improvement

1. Have a mental goal—In the Ivy League study, the 10 percent of the class that had mental goals outperformed the other 87 percent of the class.

> Successful people keep moving. They make mistakes, but they don't quit.
> Conrad Hilton, founder, Hilton hotels

2. Start a savings plan—There is a strong correlation between net worth and self worth. As your net worth increases, so do your choices. Having a plan reduces the stress of being without a plan.

3. Law of compensation—Do more than is expected. Arrive early at work and stay late. Never sit around watching the clock. Increase your productivity. Never burn a bridge.

4. Obtain knowledge—Read thirty minutes a day about your field of work. Become an expert at what you do; it can double your income. Turn your car into a university on wheels by listening to tapes on self-improvement.

5. Time management—Organize your time to do more activities toward your mental goals:
   - Prioritize each day and month. List the activities in front of you and rank them in order of importance. Do the most important things first, then tackle the next, and the next. Re-rank them first thing each morning.
   - Power block to control your time and day. Power block is a period of time that lets you execute your activities without interruptions. Establish a four-hour time block each day. During the power block, don't let others invade your time.

115

- Delegate and eliminate. Make sure you maximize your talent. Don't do things that others can do for you. Don't take on activities that detract you from your long-term mission. Learn to say no.

- Create accountability groups and set time lines for projects to be finished. Meet with others who have similar interests. Be sure to complete projects on time. Deadlines with accountability produce results.

- Eliminate procrastination, it causes stress. The longer you wait the higher the stress. The higher the stress the lower the quality of the output. The sooner you start and complete a project the better you feel.

External and Environmental Self-Improvement

6. Observe your family and peer group:

   Are they a positive or negative influence on your life? Ask them what they plan to accomplish. Are they supportive of your new activities? If not, slowly add positive people to your environment. Spend less time with negative people.

7. Observe successful people and model yourself after them. Repeat their activities and you will soon have what they have. It may take time, but it works.

8. Obtain a mentor. Meet with a successful person and ask them for help. Ask them how they became successful. Meet with your mentor at least once a month and report your progress. Form or join an accountability group. Don't let your mentor down.

> *He who walks with the wise grows wise, but a companion of fools suffers harm.*
> Proverbs 13:20 (NIV)

Intangible, Internal Self-Improvement

9. Take control of your mental attitude. Internal self-talk is a key to self-improvement. It's estimated that by age eighteen you have been told "no," or "you can't do that" about 600,000 times. It's important to re-program your brain by filling it with positive affirmations. Look at the glass as being half-full and rising rapidly instead of half-empty and dropping fast.

> *Your thinking determines your actions, and your actions determine your rewards.*
> Anonymous

10. Write down your goals. Sign a personal contract with yourself. There is an intangible power in a written goal. Remember the 3 percent who

wrote down their goals and outperformed the other 97 percent.

11. Read your goals twice daily, once in the morning and again before you retire that evening. Reviewing your goals will remind you of your road map and creates positive reinforcement.

12. Visualize the outcome. See your goals as being accomplished. Be-do-have. Sense the feeling of accomplishment.

13. Know it's going to happen. Belief supercharges written goals. Add desire, faith and belief and written goals happen faster. The stronger your belief, the faster the outcomes.

14. Follow the flash. When ideas pop into your head, write them down right away. Don't give them a chance to escape. Follow the idea immediately. Trust your intuition. Intuition is gender neutral.

> *Visualization has been critical to my success. I'd close my eyes, visualize in my mind's eye being No. 1 on the best-seller list. Visualization will move you closer to your goals. It's done it for me.*
> Jack Canfield, co-author of "Chicken Soup For The Soul"

15. Pursue your passions. Identify the activities that get you excited. These are your talents and you should pursue your talents. Identify things that drag you down. Keep a journal and write down the time you spend in each area. Increase the time you spend in energy gaining activities. Eliminate as many energy draining activities as possible.

> *Expectations tend to be self-fulfilling.*
> Eleanor Roosevelt, first lady

16. Give back to others. The more you give and share with others, the more you will have. Create a legacy. When you get a purpose greater than yourself, you will get help from many places.

As you walk the stairs of self-improvement it is important to take integrity with you. If your actions are not based on the universal principles of right and wrong, you will fall down the stairs. The higher the climb, the tougher the fall. It can take a career to become a hero, and ten minutes to become a zero.

> *Real joy and happiness come far more from what you do for other people than from what you do for yourself.*
> Anonymous

Each action you take, or thought you think, is either positive or negative. The more positive the actions and thoughts, the faster you climb the stairs of Maslow's hierarchy of needs.

The more negative the action and thoughts, the slower the pace of growth. If you are feeling stuck at a certain level,

> *Whenever you are able to do a thing, though it can never be known but to yourself, ask yourself how you would act were all the world looking at you, and act accordingly.*
> President Thomas Jefferson

review your most recent thoughts and activities. Re-focus on the desired result, re-engage in the right thinking mode and move forward using positive action.

It would be great to jump to the top of the stairs, but my observation is that it rarely happens. As you take each step, it is necessary to integrate and digest each level, and make it a daily habit. The integration helps you climb the next step when you are ready.

The intangible parts of self-improvement may be quite a stretch for first time readers. They were for me, too. But as I kept reading and experimenting, I found the principles to be true. I used each step and have experienced the rewards of the process. You can, too, if you take the first step.

> There is only one corner of the universe you can be certain of improving, and that's your own self.
> Aldous Huxley, writer

Cause and effect is the key to any outcome. Choose a mental goal and you're on the first step of exponential compounding. The choice is yours.

Exponential compounding is extremely rewarding but it won't be easy. There are always barriers along the way; here are a few I experienced.

Barriers of Self-Improvement

1. Attitude. If you can't control your attitude, you are doomed by your own internal self-talk. Change your thinking and you will change your results.

2. Family and peer groups. Watch out and steer away from people with negative attitudes and speech. They can pull you down and hold you back.

3. Fear of failure. Always doing just enough to get by. Bouncing on the bottom tier of your comfort zone.

4. Fear of success. "Wow, this self-improvement stuff is working. Hope they don't expect me to do it all the time. I'd better move back into my own comfort zone." Or, "I don't deserve success so I'd better move back into my own comfort zone."

5. Fear of having it all. Do you have the courage to change? Can you pursue your passions and create a legacy? Now that you are self-actualized, what is your true purpose in life?

Whenever I feel like quitting (which has happened many times) I think of Thomas Edison and Abe Lincoln, who failed many times before finding success. The easiest thing to do is to quit. Small, consistent action produces meaningful results just like compound interest. The more positive the action and the longer the time, the greater the outcome.

American history is papered with common citizens who knew what they wanted and pursued their passions. They changed the face of America.

> *Pay no attention to what the critics say. A statue has never been erected in honor of a critic.*
> Jean Sibelius, Finnish composer

We don't have to take the risks our forefathers did to be successful in America. We have it easy, maybe too easy.

The formula of compound interest is the simple financial roadmap that's available to everyone. It's free and you can't beat the price. The formula requires the user to load principal into the program and then be patient. The more patience, the better it works. When you mix the formula with self-improvement, the sky is the limit. Set a goal and reach for the sky.

Summary

- Nearly half of all Americans have saved less than $10,000 toward retirement.
- Many people won't put goals in writing because of fear of accomplishment.
- Establish a workable self-improvement program and stick with it. If you fail in any area, don't feel bad about yourself. Get up and try again until you accomplish your goals.

APPLICATION

Proper Use of Formula
Equals Financial Success

Once you've saved, invested wisely and firmly committed to letting time complete the compound interest formula, do yourself a last favor: don't let ignorance of the formula shortcut your plans for a financially fruitful retirement. The writers hand you a number of significant do's and don'ts that will help you meet your long-term financial goals. They tell you of the importance of balance, how to get good financial advice, and ways to deal with generational and legacy wealth.

I like the dreams of the future better than the history of the past.

President Thomas Jefferson

Now you know the formula. It is, indeed, a little secret that has been used for centuries to create financial abundance for any person who chooses to use it.

People who use the formula are virtually guaranteed of some form of financial success. The principles are simple, but they require patience and discipline.

1. Obtain principal. For the formula to work, you must increase your income or decrease your spending.

2. Rate of return. Equity ownership produces the highest rate of return. Although it is not guaranteed, it has consistently outperformed inflation.

3. Time. Start early. The early bird does get the worm. In fact, he owns a worm farm and hires grasshoppers and rabbits to run it.

4. Minimize your taxes. Taxes rob principal from the formula. Maximize your tax-free loan from the government and use the loan for as long as possible.

5. Become a wise consumer. Don't assume that because everyone swarms around something, it's your best choice. Don't be a follower. Often, the thing that draws the swarm smells rotten. The difference between a 15- and 30-year home loan could fund your retirement. Small amounts of money can grow into big bucks, when given proper opportunity and adequate time.

6. Debt. Never pay an interest rate higher than your investments can earn. If you are loaded in bad debt, get out. List your debt from highest

interest rate to the lowest. Then pay off each debt and use the saved interest expense to fund the formula.

7. Make a plan. People with plans have twice as much as those without one. Write down your goals and review them twice daily. Watch your choices multiply.

8. Exponential compounding. Walk the stairway to success. It doesn't cost anything. The results are magic.

The Top Ten Hazards to Success Using Compound Interest

A. Ignorance of the formula.

B. Spending more than you earn.

C. Working for an employer that doesn't offer a payroll-driven savings plan, or working for a company that offers a plan but choosing not to particpate.

D. Bad debt. Reverse or negative compounding; paying more interest than you can earn.

E. Marrying a compulsive spender. Sign a prenuptial or postnuptial agreement stating that you will save at least 10 percent of your income and live on the rest.

F. Divorce. Splits your assets. One third goes to your former spouse, 1/3 to you and 1/3 to an attorney, if you're lucky enough to share a single attorney.

G. No road map. If you don't know where you're going, any path will get you there.

H. Changing the plan. Chasing returns. Moving from strategy to strategy, trying to outperform the averages.

I. Excess debt. Leveraging principal, trying to get rich fast. Debt causes stress and makes rabbit stew out of lots of rabbits.

J. Moving the goal posts. Reaching your goal and then wanting more, thus failing to create balance in your life.

> If you don't know where you're going, you might wind up someplace else.
> Yogi Berra, baseball great

The Importance of Balance

This book spends a lot of time on common sense wealth creation. It's important to state here that you don't need to become a slave to the formula.

If money is your only purpose in life, you'll find yourself missing out on many of the finer things life offers. You could wind up with a lot of money and nobody to share it with.

Whenever I listen to Harry Chapin's song, Cat's in the Cradle, it drives home to me the point of balance. Early in my career I didn't like to hear the song. I was working too many hours and not spending much time with my family. I felt guilty every time I heard the song.

There is another lesson in the song and one of the main reasons for this book. In the stairway to success, we talk about modeling as a self-improvement technique. Parents should be careful about what they do and say around their children. Keep in mind that your children are watching (modeling) your every behavior.

Children rarely listen to what parents say, but mimic every action they do. If you lie, they will lie. If you tell the truth, they will tell the truth. If you smoke a pack of cigarettes a day, don't be disappointed when your child lights up.

If you are in debt and can't control your spending, then don't be shocked when they embrace debt, too. When you change your financial ways and embrace the compound interest savings formula, don't be surprised when your children also buy into the formula.

> No legacy is so rich as honesty.
> William Shakespeare, playwright

It's said that one of the greatest joys in life is becoming a grandparent. Being a grandparent is a great position to hold; all the fun of children without the day-to-day parenting hassles.

One day it hit me that my biggest responsibility as a parent was to create a joyous environment for my future grandchildren. Whatever my children observed was the same environment my grandchildren would experience. My responsibility is not only to my children, it is to future generations. The challenge is in transferring family values to the next generation.

You can't take your money with you, but you can create a legacy of values and principles that will endure forever.

Personal Wealth:
How Do I Get Started?

If you have come this far and want to embrace the formula, the execution is much simpler than you might think.

As stated in Lesson VI, you get the most financial bang by maximizing your employer's payroll-driven plan. If you have no plan, an IRA is your next best choice. Each person's situation is a little different from the next.

> *We can't become what we need to be*
> *by remaining what we are.*
> Oprah Winfrey, television personality

The process I use with clients is reverse investing. Determine the specific outcome or goals and work backwards. Once you know the outcome and your risk tolerance, the execution or action steps are common sense.

The next step is where to invest the money. If you have a long-term goal, then equities (ownership) are your best choice. One of the easiest ways for beginning investors to start is through mutual funds. Mutual funds offer diversification, professional management and the ability to get started with small amounts of money.

Diversification (or not putting all your eggs in one basket) shouldn't be taken lightly. The biggest mistakes I have made in my investment career were because of the lack of diversification.

Mutual funds use economies of scale and combine assets with other investors. Each fund has its own investment objective. Based on that objective, the manager makes buy and sell decisions to increase the value of the pool of diversified assets.

Some mutual fund families' minimum investments are as little as $100 and will accept $25 additional payments to your account.

Research has shown that the asset allocation decision—how your investments are split among different asset classes such as stocks, bonds, and cash—has by far the greatest impact on overall portfolio performance.

Security Selection, Market
Timing & Other

8.5%

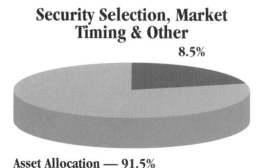

Asset Allocation — 91.5%

As illustrated in the graph, 91.5 percent of total return variation is due to the asset allocation of your portfolio. In contrast, market timing and stock selection account for 8.5 percent. This result is why determining the right asset allocation policy for you is so critical to your investment success.

There is no single, universal asset allocation strategy. The makeup of your portfolio should be based on your goals, risk tolerance, and, perhaps most importantly, your investment time horizon.

The length of time you have before you need to access your investment affects your strategy. Investors with a longer time horizon can afford to take greater risk in exchange for greater return.

Historically, stocks have outperformed bonds and other fixed income investments over the long term, but demonstrated greater short-term volatility as well.

Here are some commonly used allocation models based on various investment objectives.

Asset Allocation Models to Meet Your Needs

80% Fixed Income

20% Equity

Income investors are conservative investors who place considerable value on a significant and relatively stable income stream and whose requirement for wealth enhancement is clearly secondary. They want both the stability of income and a significant degree of protection from market loss.

60% Fixed Income

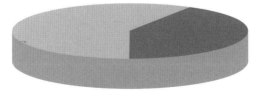

40% Equity

Income and Growth investors are moderately conservative investors who want to emphasize income and stability of principal in their portfolio, but at the same time maintain some potential growth.

40% Fixed Income

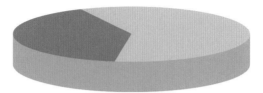

60% Equity

Balanced Growth investors are interested in total return and use income to reduce risk. They want to preserve the real value of their capital while achieving an income stream from it. They understand that this goal requires assuming at least a moderate risk.

20% Fixed Income

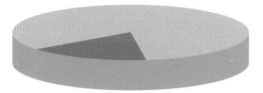

80% Equity

Growth investors are total return investors who are primarily interested in capital appreciation and are willing to take visible risks to achieve their goals. Current income is clearly a secondary concern.

100% Equity

Aggressive growth investors want to build significant wealth over time. They are interested in allocations that offer the potential for high returns despite the possibility of substantial variability of investment returns.

In 1992, there were 21 defined investment categories. Now there are hundreds. In 1993, when Peter Lynch of Fidelity Magellan fame wrote his book,

Beating the Street, there were 3,565 mutual funds. Six years later, the number had increased to over 11,000.

Each asset class has a different investment style described in the prospectus. Various equity styles include:

Large Cap Growth	**Large Cap Value**
Small Cap Growth	**Small Cap Value**
International Growth	**International Value**
International Small Cap Growth	**International Small Cap Value**

Since predicting what style is going to be in favor at any particular time is virtually impossible, it's important to have a portfolio that has exposure to different styles.

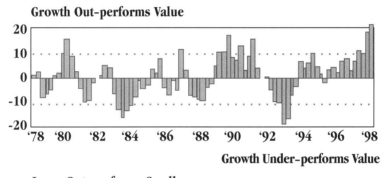

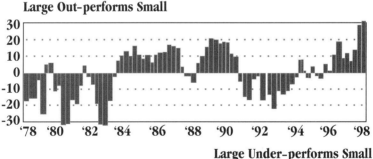

Should You Pay for Advice?
Whether to Hire an Advisor

Good, solid advice costs money, there's no doubt about it. If you spend time reading and studying the financial services industry, over time you can become an expert. But be prepared to spend several years in the learning process. Otherwise, it's wise to choose an experienced advisor.

There's so much financial information being created that you'd have to be Rip van Winkle not to have heard anything about the investment industry during the last couple of years.

As the learning process progresses, terms that once frightened and intimidated beginners gradually lose their power and become common knowledge. It's fun to watch novice investors get their financial legs and start to ask probing financial questions. If investing becomes a hobby and you take control of the investment process, the mental and financial rewards are extremely exciting.

If you don't want to read the financial press and become glued to the financial news channels, then working with an investment advisor is another option. One advantage of working with an advisor is the creation of an accountability group, as mentioned in Lesson IX. Should you tend to procrastinate, an advisor will help hold you accountable.

When you describe your financial goals, advisors will give you an action plan to follow and tell you whether your objectives are realistic. Once a goal is set, establish a time to review the plan each year. When you get the advice, don't forget to execute. A good advisor will help keep you on track and reinforce your investment goals.

Another important reason to consider an advisor is that when times get tough in the financial markets—and they will—an advisor will reinforce your long-term strategy and talk you out of an emotional financial decision.

From 1970 to 1999 the
stock market has declined:

5%	39 times
10%	13 times
15%	8 times
20%	5 times
25%	4 times (a bear market)

If you have a plan and understand the risks, an advisor will make sure you don't act dramatically and stray from the course of responsible investing.

Equities are the only thing that Americans won't buy on sale. When all the investment rabbits are selling because of impending financial doom, your advisor can reaffirm the financial opportunity before you.

Several studies compared the investment returns between self-help investors versus investors that used advisors. The average holding period for self-help investors was twenty-two months. The advisor-based investors held funds forty-nine months, greater than twice the time of the self-help investor.

130

Advisor-based investors financially outperformed the self-help investors because they spent more time in equities.

Peter Lynch said he has never met a short-term investor; everyone he asks claims to be investing for the long-term.

There is a disturbing trend that more and more people are having a hard time sticking to long-term investment plans. The constant flow of financial information doesn't stop. With 24-hour financial news channels, more than 150 financial publications and a rapidly growing internet, the deluge of investment double-talk can create doubt for any investor.

Before investing use the following contract to hold yourself responsible to your financial goals. If you want to maximize your return and aren't committed to holding equity investments for at least 10 years, statistically you are gambling, not investing.

INVESTMENT CONTRACT

1. Investment Objectives

❑ Growth

❑ Safety

❑ Income

2. Holding Period

❑ 1-3 years

❑ 3-5 years

❑ 5-10 years

❑ 10-20 years

❑ Other _____

3. Investment Strategy

❑ Buy Low, Sell High

❑ Buy High, Sell Higher

X _____

Signature

This little contract may seem hokey, but it is what an investment advisor will bring to mind if you are frightened and want to make an emotional decision.

The alchemic performance of the stock market has attracted a rainstorm of new investors into the market. The decade of the 90's, with the consistent upward trend in prices, has lulled many novice investors into a false sense of complacency.

People believe stocks are a sure thing. Household ownership of equities is at record levels. This level of possession hasn't been matched in more than thirty years.

As the market climbs higher and higher, the common cry is "this time is different." A new era of economic prosperity is upon us. Investors become mesmerized by the movement of the market and ignore the fundamentals of long-term investing.

How Much Would You Pay for a Tulip Bulb?

It's hard to believe that over 350 years ago someone shelled out more than $20,000 for a single tulip bulb. Ever wonder how much that amount would be adjusted for inflation?

Manias are a basic part of human nature. Whether it is a mania for the latest hot pop star or a mania to buy a sure thing financial asset, manias have exerted their influence for centuries. Unlike the lessening of the fervor directed toward a pop star, the end of a financial mania can often have devastating effects on its participants.

Tulips were first imported into Europe from Turkey in the mid-1500's. The flowers soon gained in popularity, and a demand sprang up for different varieties of the bulbs. The supply, and increasing popularity, of rare varieties of tulip bulbs couldn't keep up with the demand, and prices soon began a rapid rise.

Prices rose to such heights that by the year 1610, one rare bulb was considered an acceptable dowry for a bride. As prices soared, ordinary citizens soon began to view tulip bulb speculation as a sure-fire way to get rich (signal bell of the stock market?).

Holland, the largest producer of the bulbs, soon became the epicenter of the mania for tulips. People mortgaged their homes and businesses to buy the bulbs. The prices for many rare bulb types reached several hundred dollars each.

One bulb of a very rare variety even changed hands at over $20,000. By 1637, people began to see that prices had reached an outlandish level. Selling began to take place, and as often happens after the smart money has already sold, a crash soon followed.

Many Dutch families lost the homes and businesses they had mortgaged to take part in this "sure thing" investment. I'm not here to rain on the equity parade, but earnings will determine the long-range prices in the stock market.

If you decided to buy the local ice cream store, how much would you pay for a business that is losing money? How much would you offer if the store just broke even financially?

Private business owners put the pencil to their purchases. How much money would a bank lend you to buy a business that's losing money? Not much!

Investment rabbits tend to buy what's moving or what has already moved, paying little attention to the fundamentals of the company. Buying stocks that don't make money is gambling—hoping to hit the Big One. If a company doesn't make money, it's just a matter of time before the stock price will decline in value.

Successful investors develop rules and systems. The rules force discipline and the discipline over time produces consistent results. Systems take the emotion out of the decision making process.

One popular system is the ranking of a financial index of thirty companies by their dividend yields. List the company's dividend returns from highest to lowest. Put an equal amount of principal into each of the ten highest yielding stocks.

In one year, re-list again the index by dividend yield and re-balance the portfolio.

This method of investing has out-performed the index by nearly 50 percent since 1973. Why would this be? Because the system forces investors to buy low and sell high. The highest yielding stocks are temporarily out of favor.

When the stock increases in price, the yield declines and they are sold high and replaced by another stock that has under-performed the index.

Just like the investment contract, buy low and sell high. The only safe harbor in the market is value. Investment fads will come and go. Hot industry groups appear and disappear.

Regardless of the market direction, people that buy dividend paying blue chip stocks when they are low and selling them when they are high have a lifelong strategy that will be consistently rewarding.

Growth investing is another successful strategy that produces high returns in exchange for higher volatility.

Generational Wealth:
Use Wisdom in Your Generosity

There is a popular book entitled, Die Broke. The theory is to be penniless when you die. If you have accumulated wealth, that choice is yours.

In my family, each generation has tried hard to give more opportunity to the next generation. The best investment that parents and grandparents can make is investing in a college education (intellectual compounding) as was quantified in Lesson II.

> Teach your children to achieve, not just to consume.
> Thomas J. Stanley and William D. Danko,
> "The Millionaire Next Door"

If transferring wealth to your children or grandchildren is your goal, compound interest used over two lifetimes produces larger results because of the longer compounding period. Time is the greatest ally to compound interest.

An entire book could be written on generational wealth using compound interest. Here are a few simple ideas.

Fund IRAs for your children. As soon as a child has earned income (wages), fund a Roth IRA. If a 13-year old youngster puts $2,000 a year into an IRA and it earns 11.22 percent compounded annually until age 65, the nest egg will be $4,475,288.89. Remember, if the child's money is placed in a Roth IRA, the accumulation of wealth is entirely free of income tax if held to age 59 1/2.

Another strategy for a parent or grandparent is to convert part of a traditional IRA into a Roth IRA and name a grandchild as beneficiary.

A conversion of $2,000 at birth (not adding a penny to the initial amount) will produce $1,294,931.89 at age 65 at 10 percent interest. What a thoughtful and useful gift to leave for a child.

My suggestion is to write a letter, to be given to the grandchild at a much later time, explaining the value of compound interest. Encourage them not to touch the balance until they retire. Tell them to pass part of their wealth to their grandchildren and keep the abundance growing so each future family can realize their full potential.

Another scenario is to name grandchildren as beneficiaries of traditional IRAs. I've seen an example where $550,000 in a traditional IRA created more than $41 million spread over two lifetimes. Uncle Sam, of course, will try to get his share but you can also use tax-planning tools such as a charitable lead trust to fend off some of the estate taxes.

In the laboratory, these strategies work every time. In application, however, the variables of patience, discipline and temptation will make the execution difficult. But the possibilities exist to transfer wealth to the next generation. The greatest challenge to the parents is transferring their family values to the future generations, not the financial abundance.

Legacy Wealth
Leaves a Warm, Fuzzy Feeling

As mentioned in the last chapter, giving to others is the greatest power on earth. Legacy wealth is when you mix compound interest with perpetuity.

Lib Kimrey of Greensboro, North Carolina, will be remembered for years to come by many at Centenary United Methodist Church, where she so willingly gave her time and small acts of generosity. Mrs. Kimrey, who never worked outside her home and died in 1996 at age 83.

It wasn't until three years later that the church learned that Mrs. Kimrey had left a $1,839,739.74 bequest to the church, which she considered part of her family.

Mrs. Kimrey's parents left their estate to her with the understanding that she would will it to the church upon her death. When she died, she left 80 percent of her estate to the church and 20 percent to her stepson.

The church board spent some of the money to pay off debt on the parsonage and to pave the church parking lot. The rest was placed in a Methodist foundation, earning the church about $150,000 a year in interest.

Ben Franklin's $5,000 gift to the city of Philadelphia is a great example of legacy wealth. Most non-profit organizations spend every dime they raise through fundraising. Each year, they repeat the same process.

Committing selfless acts is a major step toward real happiness.
Anonymous

When a non-profit spends everything it earns, the organization's only as good as the current group of volunteers. If non-profit organizations were to establish an operating endowment, take 10 percent of what they receive and invest it in the compound interest formula and let it grow over time, the interest from the endowment would eventually dwarf the existing fundraising efforts.

I currently serve on a foundation board. In 1986, the total assets were $186,000. Now, thirteen years later, the foundation has over $6 million in assets and will distribute over $275,000 in scholarships. The scholarship money will never decrease. The principal and the interest will grow perpetually.

If you have saved enough personal abundance and you want to give to your favorite charity, consider maximizing the formula of compound interest. Follow the lead of Ben Franklin, and be creative with compound interest and let your gift grow for a hundred years. Restrict the accumulation to fund an operating endowment. The size and scope of projects the organization can accomplish will multiply like the wealth in the formula.

There are some great examples of legacy compounding. Who was this fellow, Nobel? What is the Nobel Peace Prize, anyway? Think of the millions of dollars that he gave back to the generations after him. (Alfred B. Nobel, 1833-96, inventor of dynamite; bequeathed $9 million, from which the interest was to be distributed yearly to those who had most benefited humankind in physics, chemistry, medicine-physiology, literature, and peace. Prizes in these five areas were first awarded in 1901.)

If you can't tell by now, I'm extremely passionate about compound interest. I definitely think that Ben Franklin and Albert Einstein were correct in their fascination with compound interest. The formula is at least the eighth wonder of the world. The more people who embrace the formula, the better place this world is going to be for generations to come.

Conclusion

The other day I read a headline in Investors Business Daily that drunk driving deaths had hit a seventeen-year low. Upon first reading the article, it didn't mean much to me.

The more I thought about it, however, the more amazing the statistic became. A tragic event spawned an idea that led to the formation of an organization called Mothers Against Drunk Drivers (MADD), and the organization put an idea into action. The action was persistent. The action (and MADD) raised awareness, the awareness gained allies and the allies became disciples.

> Great spirits have always encountered violent opposition from mediocre minds.
> Albert Einstein, scientist

Doesn't that sound like critical mass, or the Hundredth Monkey principle? MADD's relentless action has changed the way America thinks about drinking and driving. The odds at inception were small. Who could take on major corporations, change the laws in the nation, and raise the awareness that the act of drinking and driving is wrong? The MADD organization should be proud of how a small group of people changed the views of many Americans about drinking and driving.

It's been twenty-one years since I learned about compound interest. With my rose-colored glasses I assumed everybody was embracing the principles.

But that's just not the case. I watched the slow, steady shift of the bell curve to the left. I watched more people depend on lotteries or lawsuits to get rich. I watched divorce rates rise and the bankruptcy rate climb to all-time highs.

I believe that financial education should be as accessible as reading, writing and arithmetic. We prepare students to become part of the working class without the slightest bit of practical financial education.

We throw our young lambs to the financial and advertising wolves that spend billions of dollars to enslave them with debt before they have a working knowledge of the system. They face great odds from the beginning of life's financial race.

The Let's Save America Foundation

This book is the start of a campaign to objectively educate at least a million people on the value of compound interest.

> A man can succeed at almost anything for which he has unlimited enthusiasm.
> Charles Schwab, industrialist

The first dollar of every book sold will help fund the foundation. The foundation, in turn, will create objective teaching materials to be integrated into America's educational system. In addition, the foundation will become a repository for idea sharing; a bank of ideas on how to assist others.

As we raise people's awareness and aid in their education, we will become a positive force in society. As more people embrace the formula, the Bell curve (critical mass) will shift to the right. And as people start to feel the joy of self-esteem (taking control of your life) and self-actualization (finding your true purpose), the country we live in will change for the better and our win-lose society can become a win-win society. The philanthropy and abundance will astound us all.

Become part of the change (critical mass). The first place to start is with yourself; your actions speak louder than your words. Learn and share the formula with others. Form accountability groups and share your best ideas with each other.

> There is something more powerful than anybody—and that is everybody.
> Edward "Eddie" Rickenbacker, aviator

The joy you will feel helping someone else to financial freedom is hard to describe. Try it. It's true that compound interest is for everybody.

Let's educate as many people as we can. Ultimately, it's an individual choice which side of the formula you select, the darkness of financial slavery or the bright light of self-esteem and self-actualization.

Come to the bright light.

Taoism, an ancient Chinese religion and philosophy advocating simplicity and selflessness, addressed the positive influence of leadership in a short verse entitled "The Ripple Effect:"

"Do you want to be a positive influence in the world?

First, get your own life in order. Ground yourself in the single principle so that your behavior is wholesome and effective. If you do that, you will earn respect and be a powerful influence.

Your behavior influences others through a ripple effect. A ripple effect works because everyone influences everyone else. Powerful people are powerful influences.

If your life works, you influence your family.

If your family works, your family influences the community.

If your community works, your community influences the nation.

If your nation works, your nation influences the world.

If your world works, the ripple effect spreads throughout the cosmos.

Remember that your influence begins with you and ripples outward. So be sure your influence is both potent and wholesome.

How do I know this works?

All growth spreads outward from a fertile and potent nucleus. You are a nucleus."

May the formula be with you.

Summary

- Start an investment saving plan either through an employer's payroll-driven plan or an IRA.

- Decide where to invest your money, keeping in mind that over a long period of time equities (ownership) are the best choice.

- Mutual funds offer diversification and are one of the easiest ways to start a savings program with a minimum amount of money.

- Learn all you can about the financial industry. You can grasp considerable amounts of knowledge through reading and studying. If you feel nervous and uncertain, seek the assistance of an appropriate professional.

- Leave behind a financial legacy. Consider giving to future generations through your children or grandchildren, or through charities.

The Ripple Effect: Action Step I
Start With Yourself

I, _____, will embrace the law of compound interest. Starting today (date)_____, I will find principal to apply to the formula that will move me down the path of financial abundance.

I will develop a common sense plan by myself or with an advisor that will use the law in my best interest by either paying off high interest rate debt or enrolling in a payroll savings plan. But I will commit to a monthly saving plan, investing $_____ a month.

I will write down a goal(s) and review them each day, knowing that written goals coupled with positive emotions produce results.

I will not harvest early. The formula works like the laws of nature. When I feel the need to touch the principal, I will counsel with someone to make sure it is my best option.

I know that anything I want in life is mine if I focus my attention on it and make it my passion. I know this abundance is mine.

_____   _____
Signature   Date

The Ripple Effect: Action Step II
Share Information With Others

I, _____, will share the law of compound interest with others. I will start with my family of loved ones. Before I do this, however, I will take two positive steps myself, knowing that being a good role model is the best way to transfer information to others.

I will form accountability groups that will share positive results and offer support to others who are tempted to violate the common sense principals.

I will encourage others to share this information with their loved ones and their friends, knowing that over time, as more people embrace the laws of abundance collectively, we will have a positive impact on the communities in which we live. As the ripple grows, we will have a positive impact on this great country, and eventually the world.

_____   _____

Signature   Date

The Ripple Effect: Action Step III
Move the Financial Bell Curve to the Right

I, _____, will share the miracle of compound interest with at least 10 people. I will objectively educate the principals of common sense wealth accumulation.

I will act as a mentor and offer my knowledge and guidance to anyone in need.

I will regularly check the progress of the new wealth accumulators and give them positive feedback and guidance.

I know that collectively, as we move more and more people through the miracle of compound interest, that this country will slowly build a positive wealth consciousness. Everybody, young and old, will have more choices in life and the ability to pursue their passions.

As more Americans move through the upper tiers of Maslow's hierarchy of needs, the thoughts and deeds will ascend to a higher level. And just like the formula, the cumulative effect of more people experiencing abundance and financial freedom will make the world a better place to live.

What have you to lose? Nothing!

What have you to gain? Everything!

May the formula be with us.

_____   _____
Signature   Date

NOTES

NOTES

Tell us what you think!

Please send us your comments,
thoughts and suggestions...

_____
_____

_____
_____
_____
_____
_____

Let's Save America!
Nine Lessons to Financial Success.
Bradley Dugdale, Jr.
Don M. Ferrell

*This book has had a meaningful impact on my life. I'd like to
share this information with you.*

**Nine Lessons to
Financial Success**

www.letssaveamerica.com

Let's Save America
P.O. Box 2869
Coeur d'Alene, ID 83816-2869